The Essential Guide to Money and Investments for Women

Mark A. Parks Jr., CPA, MBA

MAP CPA GROUP International, LLC

THE GIFT

ISBN 978-1-7333328-0-4

DEDICATION

This book is dedicated to my mother Alma Ruth Davis who taught me everything I know about money management.

TABLE OF CONTENTS

Acknowledgments   Page # i

Forward   Page #1

Introduction   Page #7

1   Chapter 1 All the Single Ladies   Page #12

2   Chapter 2 Working on Happily Ever After   Page #38

3   Chapter 3 After the Love is Gone   Page #78

4   Chapter 4 Till Death Do Us Part   Page #102

5   Chapter 5 Head of Household   Page #128

6   Chapter 6 Just the Facts Ma'am   Page #157

7   Chapter 7 Talk the Talk and Know the Rules   Page #173

8   Chapter 8 Types of Investments   Page #180

9   Chapter 9 Evaluating Investment Performance   Page #200

10   Chapter 10 Get Started! A Step-By-Step Guide

     to Success   Page #212

11   Chapter 11 Customized Answers   Page #247

     Guide to Resources   Page #258

     Glossary   Page #265

ACKNOWLEDGMENTS

I am extremely humbled by the amount of support I received in completing "The Gift." This book was made possible with the help and encouragement of hundreds of people. I will not acknowledge them all here, but in this new electronic world we live in, I will try to acknowledge as many as possible personally on social media. I must, however, acknowledge the following people here to leave an indelible mark like what they have done to my life.

First and foremost, I must acknowledge my mother, Alma Davis, who taught me money management skills my whole life, even when I resisted. Secondly, I would like to thank my sister Denine Goolsby, whom without an initial conversation with her, the idea of this book would not exist. Next, I must thank my amazing wife Connie, who helped and encouraged me throughout this project. Also, my sons Mark III and Charles for your continued support and my niece Devin Ashley for reigniting the flame with your personal story. Obviously, I love you all very much!

The following individuals provided their extensive knowledge and professional experience to make this book a better read. First, we have John Hayes, famed author and the Titus Chair for Franchise Leadership at Palm Beach Atlantic University. Thanks, John for your guidance on how the process really works. Then, we have my friend and library executive Kacie Armstrong, Executive Director of the Euclid Public Library and Sydnee Newman, Executive Director in the legal arena, thank you for being willing to read my work and offer guidance. Thank you Brandyce Stephenson, of BS Soul Works, for the marketing and spiritual guidance. TaRhonda Harvey, of Kolmio Global, I want to thank you for your patience and guidance with my online presence and website as well as guiding me on how to portray the best images. And last, but certainly not least my editor Malory Wood of The Missing Ink Writing Services for your editing and content service. This phenomenal group of women and John :-) really contributed to the quality of this book.

Finally, I would like to thank the following women for providing unwavering support during this project. Shalonda Warren, CEO of the Sickle Cell Foundation of Palm Beach, I thank you for your tough love in telling me to get busy and finish the book. I don't know if I would be here at this point without your encouragement. Jeri Muoio, Mayor and Kathleen Walter, Director of Media and Communications for the City of West Palm Beach, I thank you for your encouragement and support. Without you, it would have been hard to press through to completion.

This book has been my life's work. I hope it helps someone have a better life.

Mark

Forward

I was motivated to write this book many years ago when I sat down with my sister to discuss her financial plan. I had just become a professional financial advisor, and my sister Denine was one of the first clients I presented my financial consulting services to without my manager. Denine is seven years older than I so this was the first time I found myself in the position of attempting to advise her, it was a big deal for me to be able to help my older sister. It made me feel like all of my hard work and studying was paying off. Denine is well-educated, she has always had a great career, and honestly, she has always had her life in order. She let me advise her because she knew how hard I worked and how knowledgeable I was about money.

When I began the preliminary questions portion, I remember asking Denine about her investment portfolio and her financial plan. I was a little surprised she didn't have either. At the time, she was an elementary school principal and had made a significant amount of money.

"Denine, why don't you have a financial plan or an investment portfolio?"

"I don't know anything about investments..."

"Well, why didn't you get a financial advisor?"

"Honestly, I don't know where to start. What questions to ask. Who to trust."

"Great, now you do. You have me."

This was a very eye-opening moment for me because I have always admired my sister and followed in her footsteps. I later reflected upon our conversation and wondered to myself, *how many other women might be in this situation?* I decided to do some research, which eventually led to this book. I found there were MANY educated and successful women who were in the same situation. Money management and investing just wasn't something they focused on; they were solely focused on their chosen professions.

Once I decided to write the book, I thought about how I could write a book about something many women wanted to understand, but quite honestly, may not want to read about. How could I make the book relevant, informative, powerful, and interesting? How could I grab and keep the interest and attention of women regarding finances and investing? Then it hit me: they don't want to hear from *me,* they want to hear from people whom they can relate to, not some financial nerd.

***Real quick, you may ask WHY should I take advice from a man? To answer this, I reached out to Cheryl, who I met at an investment seminar on Wall Street. First, when I met Cheryl, she told me her father was a stockbroker at *EF Hutton* and all she ever wanted to be was a stockbroker.

"Mark, I received good grades in school. I took a lot

*of math classes, so I would have a strong
foundation, and in college, I did internships at EF
Hutton my last two summers before I graduated. I
also graduated at the top of my class, but when I
applied to be a stockbroker at EF Hutton, they told
me I was too young and plus, 'You're a woman.' I
went to a few more brokerages and they made me
job offers. When EF Hutton found out someone was
willing to hire me, they made me an offer, and I
took it."*

*"You know Mark, when I started in this business
over thirty-eight years ago, ten percent of the
brokers were women. Do you know how many it is
now?"*

"I don't know Cheryl, thirty percent?"

*"No Mark, it's fifteen percent. Thirty-eight years
later! We have made gains, but not a lot."*

For those of you too young to remember, *EF Hutton* was a
very popular stock brokerage until 1988 when they closed
after the market crash in 1987. Most will remember their
commercial: *"When EF Hutton speaks, People listen."*

*"I asked Cheryl, "I've told you about my book. Do
you think women would be better served by
another woman? Should women seek to be advised
by a woman?"*

"Absolutely not, Mark. I think women and

everybody else should seek the best advisor for them. They should work with someone they are comfortable with, just like if it were a doctor. The fact that you have done so much research specifically for women is a plus, but clients still need to feel comfortable with you."

So, I went on a journey to enlist women to share their stories, *"Woman to Woman,"* with the goal of helping each other. It was amazing how many women wanted to participate in sharing their stories. Some had it all together, and some were in poor financial shape and needed help. Of course, there were those who fell somewhere in the middle.

It was often stated, "If somebody can be better off because I have shared my story, then I will share."

I added my expertise in examining the women's stories and made suggestions on how they can improve their financial situations, which will be helpful if you are in a similar situation. These situations can range from what to do with your money right out of college, how to manage money as a professional, a wife, a divorcee, even as a widow.

A brief background on my expertise: I am a CFO of a major city in South Florida. I have owned a financial services company that has helped hundreds of individuals and companies with investments, financial strategies, accounting, and organizational design for over twenty-five years. I also served as the financial expert for the CBS affiliate in Cleveland, Ohio, *WOIO*, informing audiences about the impacts of the financial markets on their finances and I have spoken at hundreds of financial seminars including periodic **Women and Investing Seminars.** My extensive knowledge, experience, and caring approach has helped me get access to women who willingly share concerns about their most challenging financial issues and trust me to help guide them through their challenges.

The good thing about having so many real-life stories is everyone can find a story they can relate to. Each chapter has at least one story of a woman who has done almost everything right financially to give you an example of what that looks like. This book serves to be your motivation to achieve this feat in your own life. Financial freedom when achieved, can provide an amazing lifestyle, and you can achieve it!

In addition to these life-changing testimonials from real women around the country, I have added information to reveal the facts about why you *must* invest your money! I also reveal how I was able to obtain relevant information from hundreds of women to gain insight into how to really help you identify money challenges and correct the challenge to get on the right track. I explain in laymen's terms the complex language of money. I explain 401Ks, mutual funds, stocks and bonds, annuities, and many more investment terms. And most importantly, I give a step-by-step guide on how to get *your* financial life in order, the ultimate win.

What I don't do is make specific investment recommendations. I read a book where the author made recommendations on *where* to invest. In my opinion, that's irresponsible. Consider this: the top companies on Wall Street at the time I am writing this book are Facebook, Amazon, Netflix, and Google. When the book I am referring to was written, they recommended investing in companies like IBM. The top companies I just referenced didn't even exist yet and they may not exist years after this book is released. Investments need to be *individualized*. There is no one-size-fits-all approach.

Introduction

It's all about empowerment

"What material success does is provide you with the ability to concentrate on other things that really matter. And that is being able to make a difference not only in your own life, but in other people's lives." --Oprah on the benefit that money provides

Effectively managing money and investing are concepts most people won't argue against, but many people never learn how to invest successfully. Like other areas in our lives, physical fitness for example, unless you have a powerful reason WHY to be fit, like maintaining your health, you may not work out at all. Investing is no different. A suggestion that you should invest just to be prepared for retirement alone may not be a strong enough reason to change your lifestyle to focus more on investing. One of the most powerful reasons to read this book is to help you identify your WHY it's important to manage and invest money successfully to motivate you to get started. After speaking with hundreds of women, it is very clear the WHYS need to outweigh the WHY NOTS.

Many women have apprehension about investing and they

need a strong reason WHY they should begin the process. Several women interviewed for this book expressed their personal WHY as their children. They wanted to make sure their children would have money for college, but also a high quality of life in general. Wouldn't it be great to have enough money to allow your children to go to the college of their choice whether it's an Ivy League school or somewhere abroad?

Another strong WHY is independence. As I am writing this book, there is a large movement called *"#metoo"* where thousands of women are expressing, they have been exposed to negative situations and an environment where it is clear the "HAVES" have a clear advantage over the "HAVE NOTS." Given this environment, which is not a new concept but just more socially exposed, it is more important for women to gain their independence through having financial prowess.

There are few more liberating things in life than possessing enough money to eliminate the need to accept jobs, mates, or anything else that doesn't allow you to live your desired lifestyle.

Another reason WHY is as women are becoming more involved in the work world, they are becoming powerful and savvy in all aspects of business, yet sometimes this does not spill over into investing. The strong knowledge of investing and financial issues will make women much more powerful. Finance is the language of business: the more you understand, the better off you will be.

Another WHY is the current environment for retirement. Today, many middle age and older workers had parents who received pensions. The pensions I am referring to are formally known as *"defined benefit plans"* where the employer and in some cases, the employee, contribute. When the employee retires, they receive a guaranteed amount of income for the remainder of their life. Most jobs no longer offer pensions. Most employers now offer 401K plans. With a 401K plan, the employee contributes money and, in some companies, the employer matches the employee's contributions. There are no guarantees regarding what the amount of your payout will be and when its depleted, that's it. Unfortunately, if you choose to not participate in the 401K plan, you will not have any retirement benefits from your job upon retirement. This new phenomenon is still not well understood because the Boomer generation is just beginning to experience it.

Many of you may recall the Social Security Administration starting to send statements to people showing what their Social Security Benefit are estimated to be. Why are they doing this you may ask? They want to alert people if they are relying on social security only, they may not have enough money to retire. Retirement in the past included social security and pensions. The Social Security Administration wants to be responsible and let you know well in advance you may need to obtain additional savings for a comfortable retirement. For instance, I have made a decent amount of money in my life, but my Social Security is estimated to be less than $2,000 per month. Based on my current lifestyle, that amount of money would be highly insufficient. Think about your current lifestyle and your current monthly expenses. How would that amount work for *you*? Maybe this represents a WHY for you?

So, what are the WHY NOTS? Through all my conversations, I have yet to come across one woman who suggested she *shouldn't* invest. I did come across several "Not nows." Some of the "Not nows" were because they were "Too young, no need to worry about it this early. I'm living for the moment. I don't want to hinder my fun and my lifestyle by restricting my usage of money." These are legitimate points and it is common for young people to have a short-term view of life. If this book fulfills its purpose, it will contrast the viewpoints of the younger versus older women.

The older women who started investing late stated regretfully they wished they had started investing earlier. The other "Not nows" are derived from those who don't want to invest while stock prices are high because the economy is strong, or the economy is not going well, and they don't won't to invest because the market is too volatile, and they could lose money. My years of investment experience suggest if you invest a fixed amount monthly, which is called *dollar cost averaging,* you will succeed in fluctuating markets whether high or low; therefore, the time to invest is **NOW**.

This book will explore many real-life situations for women, whether they are not investing at all, or they have strong knowledge of investing and have branched out to diversified investments. I will provide recommendations all women can use to improve their current financial situations and stabilize their future.

The unfortunate reality is some of the stories touch on tragic situations some women encountered. Some were prepared for life to happen, and some were not. I want to make sure you are aware of the crises that can happen due to improper management of your financial affairs and offer some winning solutions on how the crises can be avoided altogether.

As a finance professional, I often tell people, "You work hard for your money, so you should make sure your money is working hard for *you* by effectively investing for better results." This makes perfect sense to me, but through my many conversations and personal experiences, it is clear many women will take care of everybody else before they will take care of themselves. Therefore, I am offering this "Gift" of knowledge I gained, from woman to woman, of solid information to assure women can thrive and have successful financial outcomes for years to come.

The goal of this book is to prepare you to maximize your financial situation while providing you real-life testimonies from all types of women and lifestyles that represent all women and lifestyles.

CHAPTER 1

ALL THE SINGLE LADIES

"A woman who looks and smells good; dresses and speaks well; loves and laughs often; is kind and giving; has drive and ambition; has confidence and class; fears no one but God; and is about her business... She's Winning!--Women by Choice

Lisa – Young and Free

When I first met Lisa, she was one of those women who is a very vibrant and bubbly young woman. She laughs a lot and seems to enjoy life to the fullest. She is in her twenties, single, with no children. She lives on her own and currently works as a secretary. She seems to be very comfortable in her skin. I recall seeing Lisa arrive to an outdoor concert alone, with her picnic basket, blanket, and a bottle of wine. She appeared to be perfectly comfortable alone in her own space. Incredibly still in this day and age, women may not be perceived to have interest or knowledge of financial and investment topics. However, Lisa is extremely financially and career conscientious and always tries to do what is best for her employer and in general.

Lisa and I work in the same building and see each other often and have friendly banter back and forth. One day, I asked Lisa to meet to talk about her investment habits. She laughed and said, "You know I don't have anything, right?" Lisa knew I am known as the "Money Man" in the building, so she was comfortable having a conversation about investing.

Lisa and I went to lunch at a local restaurant and began the conversation. We exchanged a few pleasantries and then began to talk about the subject at hand. Lisa was quite astute about personal finance and very opinionated. I asked her about her investments to which she replied, "I don't have any."

As we continued to talk, it was clear she had thought through her financial situation, and her methods were objective. One example was that she had analyzed the difference in the cost to buy a car versus taking Uber.

She revealed, "I added all the costs associated with owning a car including the monthly payment, gas, insurance, and repairs and compared it to the cost to take Uber where I typically go. After the analysis, Uber made more sense for me financially."

This is the type of analysis many people could benefit from.

How many of us do this type of analysis?

Although Lisa initially said she didn't have any investments, she works for a government agency and is enrolled in the organization's two retirement plans. One of the plans is a required plan where all employees must enroll. The other, a voluntary plan called a 457 Plan, also known as a Deferred Compensation Plan. Deferred Compensation Plans allow employees to set aside money for retirement while lowering the taxes they pay.

I asked Lisa, "How did you choose the investments for the retirement plans?"

She said, "I'm not totally sure. It's the one that stays the same."

I asked, "Is it the fixed account which is similar to a money market account? It has low returns on investment, but it is guaranteed."

She replied, "That sounds close, but I'm not sure."

"Was it the Age-Based Investment account, also called Target Date Funds? These are funds that invest based on a standard aged-based progression. That means when you're young you should be a more aggressive investor taking more

risks. The reason for this is you have plenty of years to lose money with time to recover. Aggressive investments are riskier and therefore should have higher returns. As a person gets older, they should invest more moderately. The thinking is as you get older, you want to make sure your money stays intact, and you don't lose it. When you get close to retirement age, you should be invested in very safe investments where losing money is unlikely, being there is less time to recover. Target date funds follow this progression without you ever having to move money."

Lisa said, "That's it! I have target date funds."

Target date funds are becoming increasingly popular, especially among the inexperienced and younger investors.

Once I finished explaining to her, she *did* in fact have investments, she concluded she had no investments outside of the plans at work. Lisa also had no debt.

"I don't invest outside of my work plans because I already have enough to do and don't have time to learn investing."

I asked her, "Do you have a budget?"

"Yes, although I sometimes go overbudget."

I informed her, "This is fine, in moderation. Budgets are

like diets, they need to be realistic, so you don't put yourself in a situation you can't follow. Having a budget and being aware when you go over is a lot better than not having a budget at all."

When I followed with the question, "Why don't you have a financial advisor?" she responded with, "I don't feel I should pay someone to help manage money at my modest level of income." I asked if she prepared her taxes and she stated she did.

"When I get older and make more money, I would consider an advisor."

She also mentioned she started having discussions with her siblings about what they should do with their parent's estate and that the parents don't have a lot. She wanted to avoid possible arguments at the time when emotions are high from the mourning process and wants to ensure the funeral is covered.

"I read a book about money management in college and I might consider reading another one, especially yours since you have given me so much valuable information during our short lunch. I can only imagine what will be in the book."

To build on this notion, I believe people trust me because I handle and have handled billions in corporate and governmental dollars and maintain a reputable and wonderful track record. I am well-known for explaining complex financial issues to the masses in a way they can understand and apply.

Key Steps for Increased Financial Empowerment:

1. Overall, Lisa was doing a lot right. She was very conscience of what was going on with her money. She has a budget and she lives within her means. I would recommend she works with an advisor and develop a plan. Lisa is like a lot of people who are doing things right but may not possess a clear understanding on where their efforts are headed.

2. Lisa has started investing in her retirement plan at her job, which is a good thing. She needs to verify and understand the investments in the account to assure they are on track with where she plans to be financially in the future.

3. Lisa felt she didn't make enough money to hire an advisor. I would recommend she does identify a source for financial advice, including this book. There are advisors and resources to help through these challenges, some of which are free, some are reasonably priced.

Shay – The Dabbler

Education is the key for many to transition from lower wages and potentially less satisfying jobs to a more meaningful and prosperous life. Formal education is great, but it needs to be supplemented with life skills education. Shay was pursuing her dream to obtain a Ph.D. while she was working at a middle-level management position in academia. She also taught a few college courses at the institution where she worked whilst working at her parent's business. Her goal was to complete her schooling, teach some courses, but ultimately, she wanted to rise through the ranks in academia as a Dean or a department head.

She was a fun loving, light-hearted lady with the gift of gab. She didn't have children or any dependents, but she did have a dog she loved very much. Her ability to focus was challenged, but regardless of the matter, she was able to lead in many situations. Because her parents were entrepreneurs, she understood she needed to maximize her money. She dabbled in real estate investing, and when I refer to "dabbled", I mean she owned a rental property.

Unfortunately, a lot of people purchase real estate with no upfront education. They hear real estate is the way to go and they purchase properties with no clear plan on how to move forward. She owned the duplex during the financial crisis of 2007. She had occupied the home with a tenant who eventually was unable to pay rent and had to be evicted. In real estate, when you turnover a tenant, typically there is some maintenance to be performed, such as painting and installing new carpet. When a tenant is evicted, often the cleanup and maintenance required is more severe. Shay didn't have adequate resources to repair and quickly re-rent the property, so it became vacant and was immediately stripped of the plumbing and any materials that had value. Due to her busy schedule, the rental property became a liability with no clear way forward to maintain the property.

At one point she said, "It's like a waterfall at the house now. There was water coming into the house with no intervention."

Eventually, the house was abandoned. Understand, even when a house is abandoned, the payments and the liability still exist for the owner.

In addition to the rental property gone wrong, she also had a love of shopping and clothing. Her shopping habit resulted in a situation of spending far more than she made. This challenge was revealed when we prepared a budget for her. The overages in spending were covered by credit card debt. However, the bright spots in Shay's financial situation was her long-range potential for a successful career, and from an investment standpoint, she had a pension plan at work. Her financial house, well, other than the pension plan at her job, was not in order.

In most situations, I inform people they should be

investing, but in some situations, there are more pressing issues to be addressed first. Spending more than you make is a recipe for disaster. If you are deep in debt, chances are the returns on your investments are lower than the interest you are paying on your credit cards.

The smart move is to address the debt *prior* to investing. Here is how the high debt situation normally looks: You have a credit card balance of $5,000, your interest rate is more than 20%, your minimum payment is $150 per month of which $40 is going toward your payoff, and the rest is interest. In this scenario, it would take you a minimum of ten years to pay off the debt, **with interest paid of about $9,000!** Was that television or whatever you bought worth $14,000? Therefore, the first investment should be to pay down debt. Look at your credit card statements and you will notice your balance moves down very slowly if you are making minimum payments. A good move is to consolidate the debt into a fixed rate loan and pay it off immediately. However, this will not be effective if you continue to rack up more debt on the credit cards once you pay them off.

What should be evident is Shay's case is she didn't have a plan. Prior to purchasing the rental property, Shay should have had adequate resources to handle potential repairs and court costs for unruly tenants. She should have analyzed the numbers to understand her profit margin and placed a portion of the profits in an account for emergencies. Shay should have had a budget, which would have alerted her to the extent of her overspending.

Key Steps for Increased Financial Empowerment:

1. Shay had a lot going on: debt, rental property, and a pension plan. She needs to first develop a financial plan to direct her to her financial recovery.

2. One of Shay's biggest opportunities for improvement is in the area of spending and debt. Part of her financial recovery will have to be the development of a budget, which she will need to follow. The budget needs to be realistic and flexible enough that she can truly follow it. She will also need to add a debt stacking process to her plans to eliminate debt effectively. Debt stacking is the process of prioritizing your debt payments and continuing to pay the same amount out monthly until all debts are paid off.

3. Shay has made some mistakes with her rental property, including defaulting on the mortgage. Shay needs to determine if the property can be salvaged and sold. Prior to purchasing another property, Shay should acquire the knowledge on

what is required as a landlord and she needs to have adequate savings or low-cost credit options, such as a line of credit to allow her to be able to take care of property maintenance.

Levi – The Guardian

Levi was a nice member of Delta Sigma Theta Sorority, who I met when I spoke at the Delta's Financial Fortitude Seminar. She was so moved by my presentation, she asked if I could meet with her and help her improve her financial situation. I agreed, and we met a week later.

Levi worked in Corporate America and was on track to have a very successful career at the young age of twenty-three. I was already very impressed with Levi because she was the first person to respond to my offer of one-on-one counseling sessions. She worked in operations management and made a decent amount of money. We met at Starbucks, which was like my second office in Cleveland.

I said, "So Levi, what interested you in my presentation?"

"Mark, I heard your presentation and even though I think I am okay financially, I thought you might be able to help me become more focused with what I am doing with my money."

"Great! So, tell me a little about yourself."

"I am twenty-three years old, I have a good job,

and I don't have any children. I am investing in my 401K at my job. I also have a Roth IRA I contribute to."

"Well, it sounds like you are doing all things right, Levi. Has anyone coached you on money management?"

"No, but whenever I get a chance to listen to someone like you speak, I take advantage of the opportunity. I do this because my parents don't have a lot of money, and I don't want to end up in the same situation."

Fortunately, Levi had provided me with the information to prepare her Financial Analysis in advance and I had the results.

"Levi, it looks like you have two homes?"

"Yes, I own the one I stay in with my parents and I own another duplex."

"It looks like the duplex is bringing in additional income for you. Is the house in good shape?"

"Yes, I have a property manager who takes care of all of the maintenance at both properties."

"Levi, I have to say, for a twenty-three-year-old with no coaching, you have done very well."

"Thanks Mark, it means a lot coming from you. My

biggest challenge is my parents. They don't have a lot of money and they don't have any life insurance. And neither do I. I was told at my age with no children, I didn't need any."

"Levi, I have to disagree with whomever gave you that information. There is a simple way to determine how much life insurance you need in the event of your death."

Life insurance is hard to talk about with some people, because as inevitable as it is, most people don't want to talk about death.

"Levi, you use the acronym DIME. The first item, "D", stands for debt, which you don't have any outside of your mortgage. The "I" stands for income. Now, based on what you have told me, your parents may need a portion of your income to maintain upon your death, so we need to factor in an amount. The "M" is for mortgage, of which you have two. You want to pay off the homes if you were to die because your parents cannot afford to. And finally, the "E" is for education for your children, which, since you do not have children, you do not have to worry about yet. What was left out of the DIME calculation is burial. You want to have enough insurance to bury yourself, so it doesn't burden those left behind."

"Wow, that all makes sense. And what about my

parents?"

"Same calculation, Levi. You are in a great financial position. I'm glad you put your dreams and goals for the future in your financial analysis information."

"Yes, I want to buy more houses, so I can increase my rental income and eventually replace my income. I want to go to Hawaii, and of course, I want to buy a new Kawasaki. And one day, I would like to get married and have a family."

"Very impressive, Levi. I have mapped this all out in your Financial Analysis and I can help you get where you want to go. Oh, and by the way, because you ride a motorcycle, which is deemed to be risky behavior, your life insurance could cost more. The good news is based on some of the information you shared, you are a healthy young lady and the cost will be minimal."

Key Steps for Increased Financial Empowerment:

1. Levi had a lot going on: taking care of her parents, rental properties, a 401K, and a Roth IRA. She has completed her Financial Analysis and everything she would like to achieve is within reach. Now, she just needs to implement the solutions and update the plan on an annual basis or when there are

significant life changes, like salary increases or added expenses.

2. One of Levi's biggest opportunities for improvement is in the area of life insurance. Levi, nor her parents, have life insurance. They will need to take care of this immediately. They should both look at low cost term insurance to get the maximum insurance for the lowest cost. There is no reason to remain uncovered and place all her financial successes at risk.

3. Levi has many assets. Levi needs to work with a legal professional to make sure all her property and assets are titled correctly. There are ways assets can be titled (owned) allowing the assets to transfer to beneficiaries easier and to designate how the assets are distributed. She additionally needs to complete a will to make sure her property and assets go where she would like upon her death. She also mentioned at some point she would like to be married; she will want to take steps to protect her assets, whether it is to place her assets in a Limited Liability Company or a pre-nuptial agreement or some other arrangement recommended by a legal professional. This is not predicting a problematic relationship, just a smart

move to make sure she is protected. She should consult with a legal advisor for guidance.

4. Levi had other goals and dreams for the future. She needs to follow the Financial Analysis to fund her emergency fund and select the appropriate investments for her more long-term goals. Overall, Levi is in great shape.

Angela – Boss Lady

As we move forward to our next participant, you may start to notice a trend. No matter how accomplished some of the women are, there is usually a noticeable gap when it comes to investing. This was not intentional to illustrate the need for the book; it is the actual results from many interviews conducted on a somewhat random basis.

So now let's talk about Angela. Angela is an exceptional woman who is powerful and energetic as you will see when we review some of her accomplishments. She is a young, successful entrepreneur who has built a very strong and growing business. She has become a household name in very prominent and affluent parts of the country. She understands the deals. She knows how to acquire the clients. She will be a force to reckon with for a very long time. Angela has also written a book she markets and as a result, has become a sought-after speaker and guest on multiple television and radio shows. So, with all of these wonderful accomplishments, how about the investment notion?

First, she has done a great job at navigating success. She has invested heavily in her business and her book. There are many people who self-publish books, but many do not put the energy or financing into creating a quality product. Angela is not one of these people. Angela invested heavily into her book to make sure it is professional in both appearance and content. When it comes to her business, she has identified a need for office space for small businesses and has invested in real estate to offer space to small businesses. This is an aid to the community, but not totally altruistic. This is a move to continue to diversify her revenue streams. Given all that she has done, it would be unfair to suggest she has not invested. Women not only invest in the stock market, they invest in their businesses, their families, and their education. However, as it relates to her money, not so much.

Again, to be fair, Angela said, "I reached out to an investment professional at a major firm to invest some of my money, and he put me into an annuity and disability insurance."

> *"Wow, really?" I said. I informed her, "This is often a situation when the investment professional who you are working with is new to the business and does not possess the adequate licenses and experience to provide total solutions. The person you dealt with likely obtained only insurance*

licenses. The products you bought are investments, but I do not think they met your needs, and certainly not your objective. Unfortunately, your person only wanted to make a sale and not really take care of your needs."

The conversation was great, yet unfortunately, it highlighted many of the things I already knew about the Financial Advisory profession.

Angela also noted, "Some advisors with the big companies only want to deal with people who have large sums of money to invest, which I don't have now, but I will."

I told Angela, "This is very true. This is why I am writing this book. The number of people who feel they can't get the service of a qualified financial advisor is astounding. My experience is that many of the advisors with the larger companies only want to deal with the big fish. I know this to be true."

"I remember a time when I had a million dollars to invest and some of the five larger brokers I called didn't return the call."

A few did and said, "We really didn't deal with smaller amounts of money."

I said with disgust, "Excuse me? So, I know what you mean."

She said, "I felt people were just trying to sell me

something, anything. No one wanted to tell me what they were doing or educate me on what they were doing and how it benefitted me. I need someone who is going to take me where I need to go financially, and I *do* want to invest money."

Angela and I met a second time because during the first appointment, she was a little under the weather. At our second meeting, Angela was really interested in what she needed to do to invest. We met at her newly renovated office space.

> *"Hello Mark. Welcome to our new offices. Let me give you a tour."*

As I mentioned earlier, Angela is such a forward-thinking individual. She leased an office space with additional space other entrepreneurs could rent out as temporary offices or rent on an hourly basis.

> *"Angela, this is brilliant! When I was in Ohio, I rented temporary office space from HQ. It allowed it to appear as if I had a space in a very nice office complex for a very small price."*

One of the things I learned in business school is you *must* maximize the usage of your space. Angela was doing just that.

In a continuation of our first conversation I asked, "Other than the annuity and the disability policies, do you have any other investments?"

I have a Roth IRA with a little money in it, but I haven't contributed to it in some time."

I informed Angela, "The first thing we need to do is to develop a Financial Analysis. We need to get the baseline of where you are financially. Determine what your goals are and how to get there."

The truth is Angela, like many people, was not so interested in the slow and steady. There may not have been real interest in developing a long-term plan, which I sensed immediately.

I asked, "Do you want to move forward with the plan?"

"Well we can, but right now I don't have any money other than a few thousand dollars."

"I can work with you where you are."

"I also have an obligation to take care of my niece who needs me. I also take care of a lot of family members. I'm it, for many of my family members."

"Okay, but I want to help you understand you need to pay yourself first. It sounds cliché, but every person needs to set aside some money in an investment or savings account, just like you would if it was a bill. We often neglect ourselves and when we need resources, they're not there. Slow and steady is not exciting, nor will you become rich quick in most cases, but it is a sure way to build

wealth."

Angela is the classic example of someone who needs guidance. She has a lot going on, but she doesn't have a clear-cut plan. She knows what her net worth is, but she doesn't have a plan to get her where she wants to be in the future. I have helped many people become wealthy and rarely do they hand everything over the first time we meet. Angela has been misguided by a few in the past, so she is hesitant to move forward.

Key Steps for Increased Financial Empowerment:

1. Angela is very aware of her financial situation and she believes she can work her way out of the challenges. She needs to submit to the Financial Analysis to see exactly where she is and gauge her progress toward her goals. To see the facts in writing is more powerful than just having an idea of where she is in her head.

2. Angela is not saving now because she feels she has too many other priorities. Angela needs to set at least a minimum amount aside in a savings account on a monthly basis to develop the habit. She needs to make HERSELF a priority. Once she develops the habit, she will eventually increase the amount with

some guidance. Too many times women put off saving for themselves and never get around to it.

3. Angela was mistreated by a prior advisor, which has left her a little jaded. If she doesn't want to find another advisor immediately, then she should use the "Get Started-Step-By-Step Guide to Success" in chapter 10 to get on the right track. She can also review the Choosing an Advisor section because she's probably too busy and will eventually need an advisor.

Kay – The Numbers Lady

One of the misconceptions about investing is you must understand finance and money. Financial knowledge is helpful, but just like anything else, you can't be an expert in everything and succeed. It is important to understand your limitations and then employ adequate resources to help you where you are not as strong.

Our next woman, Kay, is a financial professional. She is the consummate professional. She majored in accounting and has worked with some top CPA firms. Her technical knowledge is superior to most as it relates to auditing, which is the primary function of CPA's. Auditing is an official examination and verification of accounts and records, especially of financial accounts. Auditing requires a strong understanding of how financial statements work and what the results should look like. Many people don't understand there are many technical areas of concentration for CPA's. During my career, most people associated my profession with taxes. I happen to have been a tax professional, but I have met many of my CPA colleagues who not only do not prepare taxes, they *detest* that area of the profession. There are others who only associate CPAs with auditing. I personally have done some audits, but it has never been my favorite area.

So, back to Kay. She is an auditor, as I have mentioned above, like many others, is not interested in preparing taxes. She also has no real interest in investing. She is very aware of where she is with her finances, but due to her lack of interest in investing, she solely participates in the basics. She has funds in assorted retirement plans where she has worked and has an IRA in addition to having insurance on her job. Kay doesn't have any children, therefore, the motivation to accumulate large sums of money is not there.

She didn't say that, however. She actually said: "Investing is not something I am interested in; therefore, I don't do it."

In our conversation, I asked her, "How much interest are you receiving from the substantial amount of money you have in savings?"

She said, "It's negligible."

I also asked her, "Do you understand you work hard for your money; therefore, your money should be working hard for you?"

She said, "I took twenty thousand dollars to one of the major banks and asked for investment advice. They directed me to their investment professional and he spoke with me for a moment and eventually told me because of the small amount, it would probably be best I just leave my money in a savings account, where at the time, it was only earning .02 %. He gave me some pamphlets to take home with me in the event I want to invest in mutual funds. Since I don't like talking about investments, it felt like a waste of time, so I complied and put my money in a savings account."

"I understand Kay. When I first arrived in the city, I had a similar experience. I had gone to the same bank and asked where I could get a better return on my money and they sent me to 'The Investment Guy'. He basically did the same thing to me. Once he found out I only had $20,000, he had no real interest in working with me. He gave me some pamphlets and told me to come back if I was interested in investing in the mutual funds highlighted in the pamphlets.

Understand, this is not a major point of interest to banks. Some banks would rather you invest your money, no matter how much in a .02 % savings account or whatever their current rates are so they could lend it out at 6% interest or give someone a credit card backed by your money for 15 - 29% interest. That's how they make their money. The banks take your money and pay you as little as possible. Then they utilize the same money to lend to others and make a large profit. A clear sign this is not important to banks is they only have a professional who comes in *occasionally* to handle investments." The message here is you definitely want to investigate options other than banks for investing.

So now Kay is even more discouraged with the thought of investing and may never go down that road again. The banks won this fight and they do this often. I will go on tirades against banks, but the reality is, they are doing what they are supposed to do. In our capitalistic system, they are making as much money as they can.

Key Steps for Increased Financial Empowerment:

1. Kay has a great financial mind, but no interest in investments nor accumulating a lot of money. I would suggest Kay read some of the stories in this book to observe how life can change sometimes for the worst and understand it is best to be prepared for bad times even if you never need to utilize the resources.

2. Kay was mistreated by a prior advisor, which made her not want to invest her money. If she doesn't want to find another advisor immediately, then she

should use the "Get Started" step-by-step approach in chapter ten of this book to get on the right track. She can also review the choosing an advisor section because she's probably too busy and will eventually need an advisor.

CHAPTER 2

WORKING ON HAPPILY EVER AFTER

"The healthiest relationships are those where you're a team; where you each protect each other and stand up for one another."--Sharon Rivkin, author and licensed family and marriage counselor

This chapter contains the stories of married women, some who have it all together, and some who are striving to improve their financial lives. It highlights the range of those who handle the money to those who allow someone else to have total control. Many of these women are professionals who make six figures or more or are married to men who do. Their challenge is: how do they know what their financial position is? Many let their husbands handle the money with blind faith believing they are doing the right thing. Others are more involved. Solutions for every scenario are included.

Maria – Scared Grandma

Maria is one of the spryest women I know. When we met, she was working in a senior level finance position in a great organization. At the age of sixty-seven, she was still the "go to" workhorse for her department. She had a ton of institutional knowledge and I wonder how the organization will ever survive without her when it comes time to retire. Unlike some elderly workers her age, Maria has no fear of technology. She learns and uses new technology just like the youngsters who do it intuitively.

In her personal life, Maria is like a saint. She does annual missionary trips to help the less fortunate. Although Marie is older, she's only been married for about ten years. Her husband has retired, and he would love for her to be home more. Because of Marie's dedication to her job, not only does she go to work, she often stays late to assure everything is as it should be.

She once revealed to me her husband is starting to be unhappy with her not being at home, so I asked Maria, who is financially very savvy, "Maria, why don't you retire? I understand your organization really needs you, but sometimes you have to think of yourself."

With a very sad and concerned look on her face, she said, "Mark, I am scared to death to retire. I don't think we will have enough money and I don't want to be a burden to my children, because I hate to say it, but my mother was to us. She and my dad had done nothing to prepare for their retirement and when dad died, we had to take care of mother one hundred percent. Because we had a house full of children and she lived in another state, we had to take care of her household *and* ours."

> *"I understand your concern Maria, but you have*
> *worked for this organization for over twenty years.*
> *Don't you have significant retirement savings?"*
>
> *"Well Mark, you have to understand I haven't made*
> *a lot of money at my level and my husband doesn't*
> *have a lot of savings either. And much to my*
> *dismay, he had us buy a new and expensive house*
> *after he retired which is really putting a strain on*
> *our finances. I've talked to the retirement*
> *consultants at my job and based on how much*
> *income I will be bringing in, I'm very scared. I may*
> *just have to work until I croak."*

Being an advisor extraordinaire, it is tough for me to hear situations that I don't have an immediate fix for, but the challenge is: when you are all the way at the end of your career, it's hard to recover financially.

Key Steps for Increased Financial Empowerment:

1. Maria has worked beyond the standard retirement age and she is scared to stop working because she doesn't know if she will have enough money. Maria needs to work with an advisor to generate a budget for when she retires. All income and savings need to be included. She can then determine if there is a situation of not having enough money.

2. Maria is scared and anxious about her and her husband's expenses, especially their mortgage. Stress will make Maria's retirement shorter because of the health problems associated with stress. If Maria and her husband determine they don't have enough money to cover their expenses, they should consider selling the house. Too often we have a "going down with the ship" mentality when it comes to houses. Maria could bite the bullet and move into a house they can comfortably afford. It's a simple decision: What is most important, health or a house?

3. Maria has always said, "It doesn't make sense to leave a good job to go be a greeter at Walmart." Maria may want to think outside the box. She is very skilled and one of the best in her field. She may want to approach her employer and other similar organizations to offer part-time or seasonal help. This would boost her income, but not require her to be away from home when she didn't choose to be.

Bernie – The Stepford Wife

Bernie and I met when I was the guest speaker at her sorority's Financial Fortitude Seminar. She was so moved by my presentation, she asked me if I could possibly work with her and her husband. I agreed to reach out to her and setup an appointment.

Bernie was a successful woman who could easily make it in this world on her own. She had a high level and very influential career as a reporter, author, and journalist. She easily could have her choice of mates and she found a great one. She found her dream man: smart, successful, educated, influential, and madly in love with her. In street terms, he was, "The Man" and "He had it going on."

No one would have known this brilliant high-level professional man couldn't manage money. For years and years of marriage, the couple struggled with unpaid debt, delinquent taxes, liens, judgments, poor credit ratings, and overall, financial ruin, even though the household income was significant.

Bernie informed me, "Working with me and my husband Keith might not be easy, but I heard what you said in your presentation, and it made so much sense. I think Keith should hear it."

It was great she wanted to correct the situation, but how was it going to be possible with him being "The Man" and all?

Could she handle the dollars and make it all better?
Could they handle an outside professional?

Could he conform and improve?

Bernie wasn't quite a Stepford Wife, but she didn't want to tarnish his image or have him feel as if he were less of a man. This is a scenario that plays out in many households and is very tough to address for some.

How dare you suggest the man is not taking care of his household?

The truth is, you *can* take care of your household, but in most cases, you can do better. I, for instance, don't do a lot of housework. And I can do better.

I've seen some women approach it like this: "This is ridiculous and if you love me and our family, you would allow us to fix this."

Bernie really wanted to get her financial affairs in order, so we scheduled an appointment for me to go to their home. When we met, Keith had to be summoned to the meeting in their dining room.

Bernie introduced me. "Keith, this is the guy I told you about. I think he can help us get some of our financial issues in line."

Keith, as I've seen many times in these types of meetings said, "Hello, not sure what she thinks you can do, we're fine," making it quite clear he had no interest in this meeting.

I said, "Okay, I'm not sure exactly what Bernie wanted to focus on, but I can go through our financial questionnaire that will get us to the baseline of where you are and go from there."

Keith was unenthusiastic at best and my attempt at reeling him in was harpooned even more when we found we were in opposing college fraternities.

The questionnaire I use is a budget form. My goal in these scenarios is to see where the money is going. Once that is determined, it is a clear indication of potential areas for improvements. Consider this: When I arrived at their spacious home in an affluent neighborhood, there were two Mercedes-Benz cars in the driveway and through a little conversation, I discovered both their children attended private schools. On the surface, this looked to be a well-heeled family and based on their careers, I knew they had significant incomes.

I began to ask questions. "What is your current gross income?"

Luckily, Bernie had prepared ahead of time based on a checklist I had provided her with in advance.

She said, "Here are our check stubs and our most recent W2s."

The information verified my assumption; their income was

in excess of two hundred thousand dollars a year. At the time, this was significantly above the average for a family of four. I recorded the information and subtracted the deductions on the paychecks from the gross pay.

"Great, now let's look at your expenses." Again, Bernie being prepared, handed me the documentation for their expenses including mortgage statements, insurance policies, and a spreadsheet with the rest of the household expenses. Initially, it looked as if the couple was just above water. Keep in mind, private school for two children approached fifty thousand dollars a year.

I said, "This is tight, but Bernie, you seem to suggest you are not able to meet your expenses."

> "Well Mark, there are some other expenses that don't fall neatly into our day-to-day expenses."

> "Okay, please explain."

> "Well, Keith is the most successful person in his family and they all count on him. His parents stay in our old home and we are still paying the mortgage. He also goes out quite a bit and he plays a lot of golf. In addition, we have a few IRS liens that are outstanding and growing."

> "Okay, let's get a handle on the total cost and let's put a plan in place to eliminate the outstanding debts."

Keith said, "It's not going to be a problem because I am starting a business and I anticipate I will be adding an additional fifty thousand dollars of income on an annual basis."

"Wow, that's great! How soon will this be starting?"

"I have the plans in place. I am anticipating starting next year."

Keith was counting on money he didn't have yet. If your mother was like mine, she probably told you, *"Don't count your chickens before they hatch."* This is exactly what Keith was doing. He was counting on money he didn't have and quite frankly, may never get to solve his financial challenges today.

I said, "That's great Keith, but what I am suggesting is we deal with what you currently have and when the additional money comes in, it will be a bonus and help you get to where you want to go more quickly."

I think what got Keith moving is when he mentioned, "I aspire to hold an elected office as a judge."

I said just to be clear, "I have been an elected official and your opponents will use this against you. The tax liens and some of the delinquent debt you have are a matter of public record. This will all come out during the campaign."

Keith gulped and said, "Wow, I guess you're right. I hadn't

thought about that."

I'm happy to report that Bernie and Keith changed their approach. They began to adhere to a budget and monitor their spending. After a while, they traded in the two older Mercedes-Benz cars and purchased two nice vehicles and Keith worked on curbing his extensive entertainment spending.

Key Steps for Increased Financial Empowerment:

1. Keith and Bernie tend to live above their means based on the belief they will continue to get increases in salary and additional income from future business ventures. The couple needs to utilize and monitor their budget. When they actually have additional income, they can add that to the budget and spend appropriately.

2. The couple has a lot of debt, bad credit, and potential legal issues. The couple needs to contact all their debtors to make arrangements and, if possible, get a low interest fixed installment loan to pay off the debts and stabilize their spending.

3. The couple should continue to utilize a financial advisor.

Ester – The Millionaire

Ester is a one of my Palm Beach socialites who is at the top of her profession. Every time I see her, everything is in place. She has a great personality and is a partner in a powerful downtown law firm. We are good friends, so when I asked her to meet to talk about the book, she agreed.

We met at a trendy downtown West Palm Beach eatery where Ester is a shareholder.

"Ester, tell me about your investments."

"Mark, sorry to say, I don't have anything to tell. I'm a little embarrassed. I know you have met with some of our friends and I bet they had it all together."

"Ester, I can't discuss others, but I will say you are not alone in having some challenges. Do you at least have a retirement plan at work?"

"Yes, I contribute the maximum allowable."

"That's great, and don't you get a share of the profits of the restaurant?"

"Well, I have just a small percentage and at this point, we are just breaking even."

"Do you have other similar investments?"

"No."

How about a budget?"*

"My husband Eddy wants me to budget and invest, but he says I spend too much money,   until I reel in my spending, we're not going to invest."

"Do you have life insurance?"

"We do, but I believe we are underinsured. Mark, I'm sorry I don't have more to share, but I just don't."

"Ester, no worries. For me, it is a matter of getting information and different perspectives. I appreciate you taking time to talk to me."

We finished our lunch and departed.

Later that day, I had a presentation in front of a group of small business owners. I was presenting a presentation I do often called "How Money Works." One of the points I always cover is the need to pay yourself first. Then it hit me; this would work for Ester. If I can get her to begin a savings plan where she regularly puts aside a fixed dollar amount into a savings or investment account, she can prove to Eddy she can be more disciplined. They had been having an ongoing battle due to Ester's spending habits. This caused Eddy to refuse to commit to investing until she got her spending under control.

The next day, I called Ester. "Ester, I have an idea. Let's

meet so I can share."

"Okay Mark, I'm excited! I appreciate your help."

When we met, I went over the same *"How Money Works"* presentation I had done the night before for the business owners.

Ester said, "That was amazing. Nobody ever explained money, investing, and finance to me like that before. You made it easy to understand and very clear. I think everyone can benefit from this. I really need the analysis that will tell me how much we need for retirement and what we need to do to be on track."

"That's good to hear, Ester. What I would like to do is a Financial Analysis for you and Eddy."

Ester and Eddy supplied me with a spreadsheet which had their budget and their actual expenses from the prior year. Clearly, Eddy had a very strong grip on the family's finances.

Ester said, "There are a couple of things you need to know. We have funded college for both of our children through the State's tuition plan. We had a large expenditure for an anniversary party, but that is a one-time occurrence. We plan on replacing our roof in about five years and Eddy gave his car to our son, so we will need a car for him soon, too."

"Thanks for that information." I gathered the pertinent

information and prepared their Financial Analysis.

When we met again, I was happy to inform the couple about the results.

I began with, "You know when someone says they're a millionaire it doesn't mean they have a million dollars, right?"

Ester said, "No, it means their net worth is a million."

> *"Absolutely, and you are very close to the threshold. The reality is, what you and Eddy have done has all been handled very well. You have plans on how to handle your debt. You have plans to set aside money for future purchases. Your home is financed at a ridiculously low interest rate, so it doesn't make sense to pay it off. You funded college for your children and you're maxing out your retirement. The reality is Ester, if you begin a structured savings plan, which I know you can do, you and Eddy will be in great shape for the future. Thank you for allowing me to work with you."*

Key Steps for Increased Financial Empowerment:

1. Ester loves to shop and spend a lot of money, forgoing a regular plan for investing outside of her retirement plan at work. Ester needs to develop the process of paying herself *first*. She makes

enough money to set aside a few hundred dollars without missing it. Once she develops the habit, I'm convinced she will save more money, thus putting the family in a position to have a great retirement versus a normal retirement.

2. Ester and Eddie have a slightly complex family structure having two entrepreneurs in the relationship. Fortunately for Ester and Eddy, the Federal Tax Code is friendly to entrepreneurs and so is the State of Florida. I recommend Ester and Eddy work with a tax professional to assure they are getting all the business benefits their business owner status affords them. They can probably structure a retirement plan for Eddy's business that will save them money in taxes to be paid.

3. Ester and Eddy have done a great job financially and it was very smart of Ester to get a Financial Analysis to focus on what else was needed. Ester and Eddy now have the roadmap and are well on their way to achieving their financial goals. Because they have children who are working and going to school, I recommend Ester and Eddy start conversations with them about their financial literacy. They should have the children start contributing to an investment account on a

monthly basis and following a budget *now*, so when they are older, they will have developed the habit to be financially successful

Lee - Legal Eagle

Lee is one of the most intense women I know. When we met, I had mixed emotions. I felt bad for taking her away from her busy schedule, but I also felt good about taking her away from her busy schedule. Lee is so focused on her career, she never takes time to relax.

Lee is an attorney and she is very intense with her career goals. She is such a hard worker, she rarely takes time out to do anything other than work. One of the objections I come across often with many women is they feel they are **too busy to focus on investing.**

I said to Lee, "I'm glad you could take a moment out of your busy schedule to talk to me about my book and your investment habits."

She said, "Anything for you, but I'm sorry to tell you that I don't know anything about investing."

"So, you don't have an investment portfolio?"

"Well, I grew up very focused on where I wanted to be. I excelled through college and subsequently law school. I became an associate at a major law firm and was quickly elevated to partner. As soon as I started working, I began to invest the maximum

allowable in the 401K at my job, just because I understood it was the right thing to do. When I met my husband, I thought he had money; therefore, I easily allowed him to manage our finances. I feel bad because for the longest time I never knew where our money was and how it was performing. I am too busy at work to think about this."

Even though her career path became more lucrative than her husbands, Lee, like many other women, contributed to the investments heavily, yet had no idea about where the money was invested.

She said, "I believed the investments were doing well and that was all that mattered."

She did not really have a relationship with the financial advisor whom she inherited from her husband.

"I don't know or really like the guy, so when he would set-up appointments, I wouldn't go. And if I did, I wouldn't pay attention. We have since started to work with a new advisor, who you and I know very well, and I trust him and feel a little better about our situation."

"Well Lee, I must tell you a story about an old friend: He, like you, was well-educated and at some point in his career, a very successful attorney. He and his wife had been married in excess of thirty years and due to his focus in law being in personal

finance, she felt comfortable allowing him to have full reign with the family finances. Her husband took a high-level political position and was fired for being "lazy," according to his bosses. Because it was a political position, much of his personal data became public. The first thing revealed was he hadn't been keeping up with his taxes, which is ironic because he was a tax attorney. Upon further investigation, the wife found out they were behind on the mortgage and other bills. Their home they had lived in for over thirty years was a few steps away from foreclosure. I tell you this Lee because this can happen to anyone. In the words of George W. Bush, "Trust but verify."

Lee gasped, "Oh my goodness! What do you suggest? I really don't think my husband would do this, but I do need to take a more active approach."

"I would recommend you and your husband meet with your financial advisor annually to go over your investment portfolio. I would also suggest the same type of annual meeting with your tax advisor or CPA. You want them to bring actual documents, so you can verify what they tell you is correct. This, at minimum, will allow you to know what is happening with your money."

Lee thanked me, and we ended our meeting.

Key Steps for Increased Financial Empowerment:

1. Lee trusts her husband to handle the money and is not aware of what is going on with their investments. Trusting your spouse is great and essential, but Lee should still have an annual meeting where her and all their advisors review the couple's finances. This will allow Lee to be completely knowledgeable and comfortable with their financial situation.

2. Lee doesn't have a clear understanding of their investments. Like the first issue, but different. Lee and her husband need to have a Financial Analysis to assure what they are doing is in sync with where they want to be, not just investing for the sake of investing.

Gwen – The Engineer

I met Gwen through a mutual friend. When I met them both for lunch, she seemed very reluctant to speak with me.

I started the conversation as always by asking, "Tell me what you know about investments?"

In this meeting, I was talking to two women at once. They

were on opposite ends of the investment knowledge spectrum. The other woman had nothing in place and had no real plans to do so. Gwen let the other woman complete her conversation, and she was fine not saying anything at all.

I had to ask, "So, Gwen how about you?" Please note Gwen is a very talented engineer, a mother, and a woman who has it all together. She has always been conscience of her finances. My professional experience has taught me engineers and math teachers more times than not feel they possess all the answers about their finances, whether they are right or wrong. Gwen was no different.

> "Well, I have been investing for a very long time. When I got my first job after college, I immediately started to contribute twenty percent of my salary into the 401K plan and I have continued to invest at least that much of my salary."

> "Wow, that's great. What I have observed is most people who do the right thing at an early age were guided by their parents. Is that how you learned?"

> "No, actually, my parents were very poor. They didn't have money to invest, but my mother did suggest to me when I get some money, I shouldn't live beyond my means. I always took this very seriously. The fact my parents were so poor really motivated me to not follow in those footsteps. I have worked very hard to save and invest my

money."

"So, where did you learn what you know about saving and investing?"

"I read a lot and I talk to friends who invest. For instance, I have reached the maximum I can contribute to my retirement account, so now I am starting a Roth IRA."

The Roth IRA is an investment that grows tax free and is also tax free when withdrawals are taken. This is a positive investment to add to a portfolio because at some point, you will have to pay taxes on most other retirement accounts, and a Roth IRA helps lower the tax obligations.

"Gwen, that is all very impressive. It sounds like you really have it all together."

She said, "I enjoy it. My husband and I have also started to branch out and invest in business ventures. We have one e-commerce investment that brings in two thousand dollars a month and requires no effort from us."

"That's amazing!" I informed her colleague who was at lunch with us, "That's an example of what is called a 'passive business activity.' You make money without any work being required. It's a wonderful thing."

Gwen and I haggled over the bill and I was able to convince her to let me pay. I did invite them out to help contribute to my project. I thought it was a fair exchange.

It was great talking to Gwen and quite refreshing to see someone who seemingly has it all together.

Key Steps for Increased Financial Empowerment:

1. Gwen has her financial life well under control. Because Gwen is making a significant amount of extra income, I would suggest she talk to a tax advisor to ensure she is receiving all the tax benefits afforded to her.

2. Gwen has small children. I would suggest start a 529 Plan or a State tuition savings plan for each of her children. A college savings plan could allow her to save money on taxes and to be totally prepared when it is time for her children to go to college. For more information on 529, please see chapter eight, "Types of Investments."

Secola – The Procrastinator

> *"Hello Mark, this is Secola. I registered for your Women and Investing Seminar and was unable to make it. Is it possible we can meet and discuss my situation?"*

> *"Absolutely."*

We set an appointment and met a week later.

When I met Secola, I found she was an extremely intelligent woman. She graduated from a top-tier university with a degree in engineering and had worked in the field for some of America's largest corporations. Anyone who knows people in the engineering profession know they are usually analytical and skeptical people.

I started by explaining how money works. One of the purposes of this book is to demonstrate, no matter what one's educational level is, that doesn't mean they know how to manage and invest money. All of the women interviewed were intelligent, but many didn't know *how* money works. Maybe I should be more detailed and say I explained some of the concepts about how money works, like compound interest, the time value of money, and paying yourself first, to name a few. This is a presentation I do that shows the benefits of time and consistency in investing. Being an engineer, Secola is very inquisitive and likes to investigate things and she likes a lot of data.

She asked, "How would you suggest I invest my money?"

> *"Secola, I would suggest I make an assessment of where you are and what your investment risk tolerance is, so I can make a recommendation tailored to you."*

> *"How much does that cost?"*

> *"It's free and I can get most of the data from you*

now and follow-up on anything else I may need to complete the assessment."

"Okay, but what investments do you think I should start with?"

"Initially, I would recommend mutual funds. Do you know what a mutual fund is?"

"Sort of."

"Well, you've probably heard when you invest you should diversify. Your mother may have taught you, "Don't put your all of your eggs in one basket." The same thing goes for investments. You will want to spread your money out, so if one company you invest in tanks, you will have the strength of the other companies to keep your investment stable. A mutual fund allows you to invest in many companies at once; therefore, giving you instant diversification."

"Do I need a lot of money to get started?"

"No, actually with my company, you can start for as little as twenty-five dollars per month. And due to the strength of my company, you can access some of the very best mutual funds. My company is on the forefront of urging those less likely to invest to begin doing so."

"That's great Mark. Let me get back to you after I

do some research."

After many long conversations and educational sessions, Secola liked what she heard, but did not invest.

Some years later, I ran into Secola at an event and she had left the engineering field. She in turn embarked a new adventure toward her true love: Politics. Her desire to work in politics is driven by her love of helping others. Also, let's be clear, there is certain level of euphoria and prestige with being an elected official and certainly she enjoys that also. The problem with being a person who follows a typical political career: life is lived in four-year cycles. Elected officials and those who follow them are at the mercy of the electorate, even though it seems increasingly more often that incumbents have a strong chance of being retained. Nevertheless, the four-year cycles are a reality.

This type of career could require an even stronger need to have a plan for investing. You need to maximize savings while you're in office or in high profile political jobs because there are likely to be interruptions which will require savings due to breaks in income. Many elected officials get rid of top-level positions and replace them with their own people. Due to this occurrence, in some areas, elected officials get preferential treatment where they have higher pension contribution levels than a typical employee. People in these situations need to assure they are aware of all the rules affecting them.

Back to Secola, she realized her political aspirations and rose to a very high level in a political position. After being displaced due to her mentor losing an election, she eventually moved to another state, got married, and began to re-establish her career. Secola has reached out to me again and she is ready to get started. Just so those reading this book understand, had Secola started investing when we initially talked, she could easily have had fifty thousand dollars saved having put away only twenty-five dollars per month. Nonetheless, Secola has started a plan now at the age of fifty and she is starting at zero.

This is good news, but in her exact words: "I really wish I would have started earlier."

Key Steps for Increased Financial Empowerment:

1. Secola started her retirement savings late in life. I suggest Secola has a Financial Analysis and a budget prepared to allow her to focus on how she moves into retirement. She will have to be very careful with adding expenses and very aggressive with adding to her savings.

2. Secola is still only contributing minimal amounts to her retirement. It is great Secola has started, but now she needs to make the decision whether she will work for the rest of her life or whether she will

retire at some point. If the answer is the latter, she will want to identify other sources of income, whether it's a part-time job, consulting, or an internet-based business she can accelerate her savings with.

3. Secola only has the minimum amount of life insurance from her job. Secola needs to purchase life insurance own her own due to frequent job changes. Having a family and no life insurance is a disaster waiting to happen.

Sharon – Proud Lady

When I first met Sharon, I noticed she was always friendly, dressed very professionally and spoke in soft, calming tones. She is a smart woman of Mexican descent.

I asked Sharon about her experience with investing.

> *"Mr. Parks, we live a very basic and simple life. We have modest incomes and we really don't have any money to invest."*

> *"How about the retirement plan at your job?"*

> *"I am in the mandatory plan."*

> *"That's great. How did you choose the investments for your plan?"*

"My husband works for some very wealthy people who live on Palm Beach Island and they helped us."

"Are you satisfied with your results?"

"Yes."

"How about debt, Sharon?"

"Well Mr. Parks, I read a book and followed a Christian guy many years ago and I have been following his investment principles ever since. His name was Larry Burkett, who was a well-known author and radio personality whose work focused on financial counselling from an evangelical Christian perspective. He didn't focus as much on investing as he focused on debt freedom, and I embraced the concept."

"Okay, I've heard of Larry. I have actually studied his work and have followed many of his principles as well."

Sharon began to light up. "I know, Mr. Parks. One thing my husband and I have adopted was Mr. Burkett's 'no debt' philosophy. Our house is modest and so is our lifestyle. But the good news is our house is paid off and we have no debt."

"That's amazing Sharon! That's got to be a great feeling."

"Yes, it is. We paid off our house many years ago

and started to save for our children's college fund. We have all the money we need for college and have started planning for our retirements."

"Sharon, that is amazing. It sounds like you have done everything right. In my studies, I've found many of the people who do well financially learned how to manage and invest money from their parents. What was the driving force behind your success?"

"Mr. Parks, my father was a very proud man, especially of the fact her parents always purchased homes versus renting. He didn't make a lot of money, but because we always lived within our means, we were able to live satisfying lives. For instance, even though my mother never worked, she prepared an estate plan. Maybe it wasn't what most people think of as an estate plan, which is typically reserved for the super-rich, but it was a detailed plan of what she wanted to happen upon her death. She planned her and my father's funeral and actually paid and prearranged the entire event."

In this book, I have mentioned every good investment doesn't have to be a financial one to be considered 'good.' To plan for a funeral and take care of all the arrangements is a blessing for the remaining family members and should make their grieving less taxing.

Key Steps for Increased Financial Empowerment:

1. Sharon has done well financially and has expressed her passion for financial literacy. She also expressed a desire to help people become more financially aware in her community. In one of our conversations Sharon shared with me her desire to help her community by training people in financial literacy. I recommend Sharon act on her desire to help train her community in financial literacy. This could be a source of additional income as well as an outlet to do something she loves.

2. Sharon and her husband have funded all their needs so far. Now at fifty years old, they are starting their retirement planning. Sharon needs to update her budget and personal financial statements to determine how much money is available for investing. She needs to update her Financial Analysis to determine exactly how much they need to live the retirement of their dreams. The good news is even though they are starting late, they have no debt or mortgage, which makes the amount of money needed in retirement much lower. Once she factors in Social Security and what her and her husband will receive from their 401Ks, they will be right where they need to be, as long as they follow the recommendations from the updated Financial Analysis.

3. Sharon and her husband have reached the age where they can contribute more to their retirement plans. At the age of fifty, people can increase the amount of money they contribute to IRAs and other retirement plans. Sharon and her husband need to speak with an advisor to determine how to best structure their retirement contributions moving forward.

Pam – Saver Extraordinaire

Pam is a young professional woman who has excelled professionally and is married to a lawyer. They have been together since college, which was approximately ten years ago, and they currently have no children. Pam loves children and when we met, she really wanted a child. Prior to this book being published, Pam and her husband have since had their first child.

Pam and I discussed investing a year before we sat down for an interview. We were at a networking event where she was venting about a woman who she felt ambushed her into a meeting about investments.

> *"I was so upset when Marge asked me out to lunch and started talking to me immediately about my money. I thought when she asked me to lunch that she just wanted to get to know me."*

> *I said, "Did you know her?"*

> *"No, and it was such a turnoff."*

"Wow, that's too bad. Do you have a financial advisor?"

"No and actually I do need some advice on what to do with some money we have had in a non-productive bank account."

Pam knew she needed to have her money somewhere other than in a savings account, but she didn't know what to do.

"Pam, your comments are very interesting and relevant to me. I am writing a book about women and their investing habits and what you shared is very interesting. In addition to the book, at some point, I want to go back into consulting and I will start a boutique investment firm with financial solutions for women being the focus. Could Marge have approached you differently and been more successful?"

"Yes, I like to build relationships before I hand over my money. I like to get to know someone. Otherwise, I could just go to the bank."

Pam and I are friends, so we have met and talked many times since our first meeting, but not about investing. I reached out to her and told her I would like to revisit our previous discussions in the past, and she was ready and willing. We met at a quaint but trendy coffee shop and the conversation began.

I asked her, "Do you remember what we discussed in the past?"

She remembered very well.

She said, "You are working on a book about women and investing. You were in the research stage."

> *"Correct and because I needed more married women, I am reaching out to you."*

Being the great friend she is, she was very excited about our conversation.

I started with the standard question, "What do you know about investing?"

She started where we left off. She said, "Mark, you know I am a great saver, but as I had mentioned in the past, I didn't know what to do with the money. I know there is a better solution than leaving it in the bank. Since we had our prior conversation about a year ago, some things have changed. At the time, I didn't know who to talk to. The person who did our taxes had begun to do some investment consulting and my husband and I had thought about going with him, but then my uncle who had been an investment advisor at a major firm retired. My uncle is now advising us, and we are in a good place."

The challenge was to find someone who she could trust. Money is very personal, and people need people they feel like they can trust.

"Pam, I am very happy you found someone to work with. Here's my next question: Do you have a budget?"

Pam has a budget and follows it precisely.

She noted, "I am appalled at people who don't manage their money well and know where their dollars are going. I have an acquaintance who doesn't manage their money well and they don't have a budget. Unlike us, they have children and they are on a collision course for failure. I have suggested they talk to someone soon, but they won't."

"That's too bad. Do you and your husband have any debt?"

"Just my husband's student loans from law school. Other than that, we don't have any debt. We are also maximizing our retirement plans and have been involved in the retirement plans at work since the beginning of our careers."

I told her about the impetus for my book being a conversation with my sister. I informed her I had identified a weakness in our country as it relates to investing. Although the book is focused on financial solutions for women, the weakness exists with men as well.

"I want to write a book that will be an easy-to-understand resource for people like you."

"I'm excited Mark. This is an excellent idea! You should take the show on the road because there is a huge need. This is something I should have experienced in college. All young women could benefit from this."

"I understand the need for young women to understand money and investing, but I also found in my research, this issue affects older women as well. The money management issue also affects the widows and those women who were totally in charge of the family money, like you.

"You're right Mark, I also know some well-healed widows who definitely could use guidance. I can definitely see the value in this book and in the roadshow."

Thanks Pam. As I mentioned, my goal is to create a boutique agency at some point catering to women and their financial needs. A no pressure approach, an organization built solely on referrals."

"This is a great approach, Mark. I know you will do well; this is such a positive approach."

Key Steps for Increased Financial Empowerment:

1. Pam has a small amount of student loan debt. Pam and her husband should explore consolidating the

student loans. In some cases, the result is a lower interest rate and a lower monthly payment.

2. Pam has a child now. I would suggest start a 529 plan or a State tuition savings plan for each of her children. This will allow her to save money on taxes and be totally prepared when it is time for her children to go to college.

Joan - The Prolific Money Manager

I believe Joan may have the absolute best financial management story I have come across. What makes Joan's story superior is the level of diligence her and her husband Jonah have exhibited. But first, let's talk about Joan. Joan is an insurance executive who is very active in her community. When I arrived in Palm Beach, Joan's picture popped up on social media as "someone I should know." I was really motivated to meet her because s has the same name as a little girl I hadn't seen since third grade. Although my third-grade companion was from Ohio, she could have moved like I did. I reached out to Joan to request a meeting and she agreed. It wasn't my elementary school friend, but she was very nice anyway.

As I mentioned, Joan was very active in the community. When I met her, she was the president of one of the most powerful organizations in the county. I was attempting to become part of Joan's organization, so that was the impetus for our first meeting. Joan, being such a high-profile individual, was surprisingly approachable. She had a great personality and now, I am happy to say, we are friends.

I would have been surprised if Joan didn't have her financial house in order, due to the business she is in.

When I asked, "Joan, what do you know about investments?" she surprised me and said, "I used to be the president of a major media outlet. We went public with an Initial Public Offering (IPO) and I led the charge. Therefore, I understand from the standpoint of issuing stock. My husband and I also have a great portfolio."

> *"Joan, that is very interesting. I have only met a few people who have actually orchestrated IPOs. That's amazing! Did you and Jonah put together your personal investment portfolio or do you have a financial advisor?"*
>
> *"We have a financial advisor."*
>
> *"How did you choose this advisor?"*
>
> *"Years ago, we interviewed a few different firms and selected our guy from those interviewed. He has served us well."*
>
> *"Excellent. I think I already know the answer, but do you have a budget?"*

Joan really lit up with a big smile. She said, "Most people think I'm insane, but when we first got married, my husband and I had monthly budget meetings."

Being a financial professional who has done billion-dollar budgets, I was intrigued.

"Really?"

> "Yes. We would meet, pay bills, and compare our spending to our budget every month. I would write the checks and track everything on a spreadsheet. If we had a purchase we wanted to make in the future, we would calculate what we needed to save each month and prepare for the purchase."

Now Joan is not the first person I have come across who has held budget meetings and strong communication with their spouse, but Joan had one story making her to my choice for best story ever:

She said, "Mark, I have to tell you a story. Jonah and I had been having our budget meetings for five years. We were debt free other than our mortgage. We maxed out all our retirement accounts and we were investing quite a bit outside of our retirement savings. The process was working well.

Here's what happened: We were in Canada on vacation and we saw a novelty cheese grater we both adored. I told Jonah 'I really love this cheese grater, but it is ten dollars and will take us ten dollars over our travel budget.'"

> "Okay Joan, so what did you do?"

> "Mark, it was only ten dollars, and we had done so well for so long, it wasn't a problem for us to buy the cheese grater."

I said, "Exactly."

"Mark, we talked about it... and we didn't buy the cheese grater."

"You're kidding?"

No, that's how committed we are. We still laugh about it now, which is many years later."

"Joan, that's amazing! You win the prize for best personal finance manager ever."

"You're funny, Mark."

"No, I'm serious. Others can learn from you."

Key Steps for Increased Financial Empowerment:

1. Joan and Jonah have done a great job with their portfolio and their financial lives. What they should start to plan for is their tax situation for retirement. They may explore starting to move investments into non-taxable investments as they get closer to retirement.

2. Joan and Jonah don't have children or any beneficiaries to leave their assets to. Joan is such a community activist, her and Jonah may want to work with a legal professional to start assembling a

charitable trust that could lower their tax burdens now while assuring their assets continue her good work posthumously.

CHAPTER 3

AFTER THE LOVE IS GONE

"I used to hope that you'd bring me flowers. Now I plant my own."--Rachel Wolchin

This chapter presents stories from women who went through a divorce. How they survived and prospered. Some of the divorcees were devastated and are now paying a significant percent of their incomes to an ex. Some were left with bankruptcies and financial ruin. Others are preparing for new relationships and need a plan forward to forgive the past, but not forget its financial impact. Proactive solutions to these situations are included.

Brittney - College Girl

Many of the women I interviewed for this book had clear plans about how their lives would turn out. Brittney was no different. I met Brittney as a potential college intern for my organization. My initial impression of Brittney was she was an extremely bright and focused young lady. She was an international student who had a great mind. Her professional life had no foreseeable limits. She has a bachelor's degree in business and was working on an international MBA from a prestigious private university. She had interest in pharmaceutical sales as well as some philanthropic endeavors.

Brittney and I met at Cracker Barrell for dinner, because as an international student, Brittney had never been to this restaurant which she had heard so much about. Brittney had a lovely accent. I asked, "Is that a British accent?"

She said, "No it's Afrikaan. I'm from South Africa."

I informed her, "When I was young, we used to sing a song about Marching to Pretoria about South Africa and Apartheid." I followed with, "Did you live through that?"

> *"Yes, and I have to say, I was surprised when I got to America. The race relations are worse here than they are post-Apartheid in South Africa. The blacks here are treated so much worse."*

I said, "Hell, in South Africa, you had the majority; that makes all the difference in the world. However, I don't want to talk about race relations. So, Brittney, you seem to be very bright and well-informed about the world. What is it you plan to with an MBA in International Business?"

> *"Well, I would like to start a non-profit to help the women in the world who are struggling. As you know, I am almost homeless, and I struggle to keep my child fed. I have even spent time in a shelter and it's very hard to keep my hopes up."* With a lot of emotion and sadness, she continued, *"I never thought my life would be this way."*

Brittney's goals and dreams as well as her potential to reach them are extremely strong. So why then was Brittney a week away from being homeless? In this book, I have dedicated a significant amount of time to relationships. I hadn't planned to go there, but it became such a pervasive part of most discussions, I had to include it.

In Brittney's case, she had married the man of her dreams. He was a tall, good looking basketball player at the University she attended. Brittney got pregnant early in the relationship and before she could comprehend it, they were on their way to divorce. By the time the first baby was born, they were no longer together. And yes, I said *first* baby. Brittney and her soon-to-be ex Tyrone separated, but because she needed a place to stay during a major weather event, she stayed with Tyrone and his family and became physically involved with him again in the hopes of reuniting her family, which produced another child.

So here we have this very intelligent young lady, almost homeless, with two babies, no job and no money.

She repeated, "Mark, I never thought my life would be like this. I'm so embarrassed."

I said, "There is no reason for you to be embarrassed. You have two beautiful babies and a great mind, with the academic credentials to back it. You will succeed, I have no doubt."

Unfortunately, the father isn't responsible and has since left the state. Brittney's biggest challenge to getting a job was that she only had a student visa. Her citizenship was tied to her ex-husband. Because of the restraints that come with a student visa, Brittney was unable to accept full-time employment. It's hard to take care of two babies with just a part-time income. So how does Brittney move forward?

When asked about her knowledge of investments, she did possess some knowledge.

Brittney said, "I had a great finance instructor who taught us about stocks. He taught us evaluating stocks is not just about analytical evaluation, but about the story. The instructor taught us to evaluate a company's story to see if it was compelling enough for the company to be successful.

It's obvious at this point Apple's Steve Jobs had an amazing story. Apple changed the way the world listens to music and oh yes, they made computers, too. Someone who caught the story could invest and feel good about it. The instructor also told us even though we should latch on to the story, we should still look at the numbers and pay attention to the financial strength of the company."

I informed Brittney, "This is the same advice I give. You must know something about the company. Does it seem to you it can be a success? Is it something you would buy? Do you buy the product now?"

This is all great advice and if followed, investors can be very successful. The issue with Brittney, which is also an issue I faced upon graduation, is in business school, they teach you about how to deal with corporate money. They are teaching you to be an employee who invests a *corporation's* money. Brittney didn't know the process for her to invest her *own* money. The good news is when she is ready to invest, she will have a strong baseline of knowledge to move forward.

The great thing about Brittney is she is a blank canvas. Regardless of how she feels about her current situation, she has done a lot of things right and once she secures employment with good guidance, she will be well on her way to a successful life.

Key Steps for Increased Financial Empowerment:

1. Brittney is unable to move forward because her visa won't allow her to work more than full-time. Brittney's first move needs to be securing a visa permitting her to have full-time employment where she can use her education. The second move is to secure housing and then daycare for her children. Once she has taken care of the basics, she should look for a job, preferably one that has tuition reimbursement and if possible, a daycare for their employees' children.

2. Because of Brittney's status as an underemployed student, she has not been able to take care of her basic financial needs. Once she secures employment, she will need to get life insurance. Life insurance is not exciting, but she will want to make sure regardless of what happens, her babies can be cared for. Based on where she has been so far, she knows the unexpected is a strong possibility. The life insurance should be straight life insurance, also known as 'Term Life,' and not something tied to an investment. Term insurance will get her the most bang for her limited financial resources. She will then need to enroll as quickly as possible into the company's retirement plan.

3. Brittney needs to get all the basics in order and then start to work on her financial plan. She will need to prepare a budget and work with someone trustworthy to develop a plan for her finances.

Osprey – The Beautiful One

When I met Osprey, she was the epitome of a young Palm Beach socialite. She had a bright smile, her hair and clothes were always perfect, and she seemed to thoroughly enjoy life. There were many times when we were at social events at the same time and her persona was always the same: warm and caring.

Osprey had a very bold, aggressive personality, which could have been a result of her working in the auto industry, a typically male-dominated profession. I must admit I was a little intimidated with the prospect of interviewing a country club maven since I started off middle-class household and didn't experience the country club lifestyle until I was in my thirties. However, for the sake of completing this book and making it as thorough as possible, I approached Osprey for an interview.

Osprey and I met for lunch at a trendy outdoor café in Palm Beach and in true form, when I turned the corner walking toward the café, Osprey stood up and flashed her famous smile and greeted me with her warmth. Osprey knew what the interview was about, so I expected her to be prepared.

We had a brief conversation about my wife, Connie, and we also talked about her new fiancé. Osprey spoke very highly of her fiancé, who I had only met once.

> *"I'm very excited for you, Osprey. Also, I am thankful to you for taking time out of your very busy day to speak with me. Can you tell me about your experience investing?"*

> *"Mark, you know I would do anything for you and it's a pleasure to speak with you about this topic, but the truth is, I don't have much to tell. A few years ago, I was living on top of the world. I had a large salary and a fast-moving career; I was living the dream. Unfortunately, I was married to a man who turned out to be a jerk. What makes this so tragic for me is I have to pay him alimony."*

> *"Well Osprey, I had heard this happens, but typically it is with celebrities."*

> *"Well I'm no celebrity, but half of my income goes to my ex. Every month, one check goes to him and I use the other to pay all my expenses. He also got half of my retirement savings."*

> *"Osprey, I am so sorry to hear this. So, are you in a position to invest now?"*

"I will be soon, but first, we are planning a trip abroad and I am saving for that."

"Great, well it sounds like your fiancé is doing well?"

"He is, but he is not rich by any means. I love him, and I am committed to him. There are some of my friends who have said, 'Osprey, we live in Palm Beach. You should marry a rich man for the money.' I can't do that Mark."

Osprey pulled out her phone and showed me some of the responses she got from potential suitors.

"Look at him Mark, I can't date him! I know it may sound shallow, but I can't date somebody like that. I understand I could potentially improve my financial situation, but there has to be some physical attraction for me."

"Oh my..." I said as I viewed the series of octogenarians and duds who reached out to her. "I would assume you would not have many problems with garnering suitors."

"Well, no. THEM!

"Wow, well your family has money, right? Aren't you a trust fund baby?"

"No, quite the contrary. My father remarried, and all of his money goes to his new wife and their

children. I don't get anything."

"Well Osprey, what are you going to do?"

"My plan is to stay beautiful, so I can remain easily employable. Agree with it or not, once I begin to look like an old woman, I think it will be hard for me to find a job. Once we finish saving for our trip abroad, I will begin to save again."

"Okay, that sounds like a plan. Do you need some help?"

"No, my cousin is a financial advisor and I plan on working with him."

"How about debt, Osprey?"

"I have no debt."

"Life insurance?"

"I have coverage at my job."

"That's good, but I always advise people to get a policy outside of their job because if you lose the job, you lose the insurance coverage."

"That sounds smart. I know you have talked to others I know. Are they better off?"

"Of course, I cannot talk to you about others, but I will say you are not the only one who has a little catching up to do."

Key Steps for Increased Financial Empowerment:

1. Osprey has experienced the unpleasant life event of divorce. As loving and caring as Osprey is, she is in a difficult situation. She has been married before and is now engaged. Osprey needs to assure she has things in place, so she won't be burned again by an ex-spouse. She could explore a pre-nuptial agreement, or she can make sure her assets are structured so an angry ex-spouse can't get to them. Osprey would need to work with a legal professional for this.

2. Osprey has lost most of her assets and retirement savings. Osprey will need to work with her uncle or another advisor of her choice to develop a financial plan. Additionally, she will need to get life insurance not tied to her job. Fortunately, Osprey is older than fifty, which will allow her to put larger amounts into her retirement. Part of the plan needs to determine how much money she needs for retirement and then she needs to get out and pursue it.

3. Osprey mentioned she will remain beautiful, so she can be easily employable. Osprey's plan to "stay beautiful" is interesting and I questioned her

sincerity, but she truly believes if she loses her good looks, she would be less marketable. Osprey should be "beautiful" for a while, but she may want to review her physical activity and her diet, so she can be beautiful both inside and out. It is my recommendation that she and all professionals also keep their job-related skills up to date, so they can remain marketable. Typically, this includes staying educated about the trends in your field, computer skills, and presentation skills.

Wilona – I'm Not Your Superwoman

When I met Wilona, she was a very serious, hardworking woman who seemed to be doing very well financially. She lived alone in an apartment in a great high-end neighborhood and she drove a nice red BMW. She worked for a prestigious organization and was well-respected in her field. After probing a little more, I found she grew up in a household in an upscale neighborhood where she was very privileged. Her mother, who had been married five times, was able to make sure the children didn't want for anything. Even to this day, Wilona doesn't know how her mom did it. She did mention her mom told her it was important to marry for money. Following her mom's advice, Wilona *thought* she married for money the first time because of her husband's chosen career being very lucrative. She married straight out of college to a young, handsome man who had completed his studies in engineering. Wilona understood engineers made a good income and was looking forward to a life fulfilled with everything she wanted and needed.

As the marriage progressed, the couple had two beautiful children. Early on, her husband was laid off from his job, but Wilona being the strong woman she is, was able to make ends meet until her husband was able to regain employment and move forward. Eventually, her husband obtained another position and the family was thriving once again. Unfortunately, after a few years, her husband's layoffs continued, and a termination pattern appeared. At this point, Wilona began to believe it wasn't the companies having problems; it was her husband.

I interviewed Wilona very soon after her second wedding. I was quite intrigued because she continually espoused how happy she was to have a man like her new husband.

She said, "Mark, I have been through the ringer. My ex-husband's financial situation had diminished so much, my children began to see me as 'wearing the pants' in the relationship."

I told Wilona in today's society, it is not uncommon for the wife to make the majority of the income."

> *"Yeah Mark, that's all good, but that was not the life I was accustomed to or nor did I want a lifestyle where I am the primary breadwinner. I wanted to be in a traditional relationship where I could focus on the family, but also have a career. There came a*

*time in our lives when the children stopped
respecting their dad because he was always home
and not working while mom was working and
taking care of everything.*

*Eventually, I thought to myself, if the children are
thinking this, what am I doing? So, I began working
two jobs, then three jobs, and my husband became
less employable until he eventually became
terminally unemployable."*

While Wilona and her family were going thorough these struggles, bills and past due taxes started to pile up. First, due to Wilona's childhood, everything they purchased was on the high end. Therefore, they had a high mortgage, the high-end luxury car, jewels, vacations, and everything wealthy people possess. Due to the sheer high-level of debt, Wilona became stressed and decided to file for divorce.

Unfortunately for Wilona, because her ex-husband didn't have any money, all the debt fell to her. Wilona spent many years trying to get out of debt, which hampered her ability to move forward..

Key Steps for Increased Financial Empowerment:

1. Wilona was young and married someone she thought would be successful and immediately began to live a high-end lifestyle. What Wilona

should have done is had conversations with her husband on the family's finances and set up a plan. The plan needed to start where they were, not where they thought they *would be*.

2. Wilona's husband eventually became terminally unemployable, causing the family to struggle. Once Wilona's husband became unemployed the first time, they should have begun to reel in their expenses. Additionally, had the family continued to have an emergency fund with enough money to cover six months of expenses, this would have lightened the load on Wilona.

3. Wilona got remarried. It's a hard decision, but due to Wilona's inability to successfully choose her first husband and given she has a higher income, Wilona should have put things in place to protect her assets and income. It's difficult to talk about, but a pre-nuptial agreement is not out of line.

Audrey – The High Roller

Success is defined in many ways, and Audrey had experienced it in many ways. When I first met Audrey, I assumed she was a financial professional because she held a high-level finance position.

I asked, "Audrey, are you a CPA?"

"No," she exclaimed. "I am an attorney, or at least I

was. I practiced law in another state and I became a district attorney for a large governmental unit. Then my husband got a new job and we came here. I had a desire to get out of the legal profession, so I got a job as an inspector general. This was very satisfying because even though I wasn't practicing law any longer, my knowledge of the law allowed me to better interpret the standards agencies and departments were supposed to follow. I really enjoy what I do."

In addition to her great job, Audrey lived in a great neighborhood and both her and her husband drove high-end cars. Audrey always dressed and looked very well kept, so it appeared everything was going well.

"Wow Audrey, that's great! How does your husband like his new job?"

With a bit of a pause, she said, "Unfortunately, we are in the process of getting a divorce."

This is always a challenging conversation because sometimes people are devastated, and sometimes others are happy about it.

"Audrey, I'm sorry to hear that."

"Well Mark, I don't know what happened. He lost the job after we had been here for a few months and he never went back to work. Instead of going out and getting another job, he decided to stay at

home and become a day trader."

"Nice, how'd that work out?"

Admittedly, I was being sarcastic considering this was one of the first things she mentioned related to their breakup. Also, my experience has shown me many people take lump sums of money they get from leaving jobs and try day trading. Rarely do they do well enough to sustain a family.

No, actually, he knows very little about money and I take care of the money for us. Well, when we were together. He made a little money here and there, but nothing significant."

"Wow Audrey, that's interesting." That lead me right into my first question: "What do you know about investing?"

"Well as I mentioned, I handled the money for the family. I made sure I participated in every savings plan offered by my employers. As a matter of fact, I have money in a plan from when I worked at RadioShack when I was in college. I'm embarrassed to say at this point, I really don't know where the money is."

"Are you sure you never took the money out?"

"No, I didn't, but I moved a few times and I think they lost my address."

"Okay, I can work with you and see if we can find the money. How did you choose the investments to put your money into your retirement plan?"

"I always invested in the most aggressive investments until I started my current job. When I got this job, my boss told me what to do."

"Really, does he know about investments?"

"Yes, based on our conversations, he is pretty well off."

"I understand he has retired and is now receiving pensions from two jobs and is working again getting a large paycheck? I would think he would have quite a bit of money."

"He does have a lot of income coming in, but he has shown me his investment portfolio and is doing well there, also. He has given me a few tips and they have worked out well so far."

"That's great Audrey! How about debt? Do you have any?"

"Not much, but when I was trying to reconcile with my husband, I bought him a Mercedes to try to make things better."

Buying the car was a valiant effort on Audrey's part to attempt to reconcile, so I asked, "Giving the man the

Mercedes didn't work? Well, I guess I already know the answer."

"Exactly Mark. I also have some student loans and some balances on my credit cards, but nothing substantial."

"How about life insurance, Audrey?"

Yes, we took care of life insurance before we separated. If he dies, I don't want our family to have to struggle. My children still need to be taken care of."

"It sounds like you are aware of your financial position and you are not in a bad place. Do you use a financial planner?"

"No, I have only received guidance from the guy at work."

"Audrey, do you know where you want to go financially and how you will get there?"

"I have an idea of where I would like to be, but I don't have a plan to get there."

"Okay, we need to work on that."

Unfortunately, the marriage ended poorly, but fortunately, Audrey had a strong enough foundation to continue to live well on her own. Now being alone, she wanted to begin to rebuild her life. She had lived well even though she made a few financial missteps, primarily the failure to plan.

Audrey's situation is not much different than others. Many people have made a lot of financial transactions, like buying a house, using credit cards, buying life insurance, and doing some investing, but they have no plan and no grasp on how it will all end up. This is what Audrey and many others need to secure: insight into where their financial situation is going.

Key Steps for Increased Financial Empowerment:

1. Audrey understands the need to invest and she is excited about doing it. Audrey has no plan about what direction she wants to go financially. She needs to develop a plan so whatever investing she does lines up with her goals and plans.

2. Audrey likes to listen to people who she believes have a lot of money. Audrey merely needs to do some research on her own as well because what is a good investment for some may not be for all. Audrey needs to make sure the people she entrusts are giving her suitable advice. She may also consider a professional advisor who could advise her on the information she is receiving.

Denise – The Don't Discuss Money Lady

Denise is a fun-loving lady with a Jamaican heritage.

Denise was a single mom who did what so many women do: she lived for her children. Her great personality surely helped her in her career, but she was also a very smart lady. As an aside, she had a quality I have observed in other women. She was very nice, smiled a lot, and loved to laugh. This unfortunately led her to not be taken as seriously as someone who doesn't possess those qualities. Nevertheless, she had a great career without the benefit of a college education.

One of her children was in college and she was back in school working on her bachelor's degree. She knew she was the heir apparent for the top management position at her job and wanted to have the academic prowess and credentials to maximize the opportunity. The year she graduated, so did her oldest son. To add to the excitement, she got married and also decided to leave for a job that offered a faster climb to the top. Unfortunately, within mere months, neither the job nor the marriage worked out.

So, there she was again, a single mom looking for a career. Because of her strong abilities, she was able to secure another job quickly.

I met with Denise after she had started her new job and she was very happy.

I asked, "Denise, when I called you, I mentioned I wanted to talk to you about my book."

"Yes, you did. What is it about?"

"Well, it all started years ago when I had a conversation with my sister about her investment portfolio. My sister is one of the most educated and successful people I know. I asked her about her investment portfolio. At the time, she didn't have one. I asked her why and without going into a very long story, what she said is that she doesn't understand investing. I thought if my sister doesn't understand investments, there are probably many other women in the same situation, so I decided to do some research about women and investing. So, can you tell me what your experience is with investing?"

As soon as I asked the question, I could see Denise was uncomfortable. It is not uncommon for people to feel uncomfortable about talking about money, especially with strangers.

She relayed, "I have no interest in investing, but I do have retirement accounts at four separate former employers. I also understand I could lose all my money, which is something I am thoroughly against. Also, I don't feel like I have enough money to invest and honestly never thought about it."

The good news for Denise is two of her children has already completed college and the other one was almost done.

As I continued to speak with Denise, she was clearly uncomfortable with the conversation. I ceased discussing money and investments.

> *"Denise, I can tell this is a touchy subject for you. How about we reconnect, and I do an analysis of where you are to determine if you can improve your situation."*

> *"That's fine, Mark."*

> *"Okay, I will reach out to you in a few weeks to set it up." We ended the financial discussion there."*

Key Steps for Increased Financial Empowerment:

1. Denise has no interest in discussing her investments, but she has investments she is not tracking. I advise Denise to get an advisor to help her consolidate her multiple retirement accounts which will allow her to monitor them more closely. This is important because occasionally companies go out of business or are acquired, and retirement savings are lost.

2. Denise is on her own and may be for a while. She needs to develop a financial plan based on her current situation to assure her finances are where they need to be.

3. Denise has changed jobs a few times over the past few years causing some income instability. Denise needs to make sure she has an emergency fund to get her through those periods of potential unemployment.

CHAPTER 4

TILL DEATH DO US PART

"For many women, becoming a widow does not just mean the heartache of losing a husband, but often losing everything else as well."--Cherie Blair, Wife of former Prime Minister Tony Blair

Beatrice – The Broken Widow

Mrs. Harris was not interviewed specifically for this book, but her story is one that needs to be told. When I worked as a full-time financial advisor, one of my agents brought a case to me of a friend's mother who she said was in trouble.

The agent Linda came to me and said, "Mark, my friend and her sisters called me, and they are very worried about their mom. They said she just got out of the hospital and her financial situation is causing her a lot of stress."

"Okay, did you set up an appointment with her?"

"Yes."

"And do you know what the issue is?"

"She said her father worked at the steel foundry for over thirty years but now they are refusing to give her mother any of his pension and she fears she will end up being homeless."

"Okay."

When Linda and I arrived at the house, I was pleasantly surprised. The house looked like a model home and it was very well kept. There have been times when I have walked into bad situations and the homes reflected the dire circumstances. This was not the case with Mrs. Harris.

"Hello Mrs. Harris, I'm Mark and Linda told me you are having some challenges with your husband's pension. Can you tell me what's going on?"

"Well Mark, my husband was a very hardworking man and I am so proud of what we were able to accomplish. We come from a modest lifestyle, but we were able to put all our children through college and provide a great home. You see, I am a registered nurse and my husband had a great job at the steel mill. I loved my husband dearly, but he always left the finances and household administration up to me. My husband was in the

union, but he wasn't the type to pay close attention to anything other than what directly affected his job."

I started to wonder where all of this was going.

"Well, what happened Mark is when it was time for him to retire, he wasn't paying attention and therefore didn't understand the correct way to set up his pension."

At this point, I already knew what was coming next.

"He set up his pension to be paid out on a single-life, so when he died it meant I didn't get anything. And you see Mark, he died within weeks of retirement and shortly after he died, I was diagnosed with cancer. I just had surgery and I don't have enough money to sustain myself and I can't work."

"Mrs. Harris, I am so sorry to hear this."

She said, "I have contacted my lawyer and am working with them, but Linda told my daughters you were a brilliant advisor and CPA, so I thought we should call you."

"Mrs. Harris, I appreciate the kind words, but this is outside of the scope of what I do. So, continue to work with your attorney and if you do get the money and need help structuring it so it can be maximized, give me a call."

She said, "Thank you, Mark. I appreciate you coming to

help."

Key Steps for Increased Financial Empowerment:

1. Mrs. Harris had a bad situation because her husband had signed up for a single-life payout. The way the single-life payout works is it pays one person, the owner, a benefit and when that person dies, the benefits stop. Because the payout is for only one person, the payout is higher on a monthly basis. Perhaps Mr. Harris understood he would get a higher payout and since his wife still worked, he figured they would be okay. My guess is he didn't expect to die weeks after retirement. Perhaps he wasn't paying attention. Mrs. Harris, knowing the type of person her husband was, probably should have worked with him to make sure he did the right thing. The good news is since this happened, it is now required by law the spouse signs off on retirement papers. This legislation was not a result of his case, but underscores this probably happened often.

2. This is a horrible situation to be in at a point when it may be too late to correct the situation, so what to do? What needs to be done in all households is to have discussions around money. Prior to retiring, Mr. Harris and his wife should have sat

down with an advisor to consider every move for retirement.

Elle – The Preacher's Kid

This story requires more of a back story... *Due to the significant financial implications of becoming a widow, these stories were included, but due to the sensitive nature of the issue at hand, observations were used instead of a formal interview.*

It was another extremely hot July day in Cleveland, Ohio and Elle was happy she could leave work and escape to her apartment where she had air conditioning. That was the one small benefit of living in such a bad neighborhood. At the end of her half hour drive from her job downtown, Elle pulled into the parking lot of her apartment complex and passed the boys playing basketball in the streets. The boys refused to go to the designated basketball courts down the street, so they just put a hoop in the street and played. It's not their fault the basketball courts were not maintained well and when they were, larger boys from other neighborhoods dominated the courts.

Elle got out of the car and hustled her little baby in the house to avoid the verbal harassment from the teenagers. Elle felt very fortunate her job provided daycare. The daycare at work allowed her to pick up her son Ron without having to go out of her way. This really helped since she had worked a full day at her job as a secretary and had to feed her two-year-old son, play with him and then put him promptly to bed so she could take a short nap. Ron was a great kid. He had no idea about the struggles they were going through. He was just happy to be with his mom. He was the spitting image of his dad who Elle loved very much, so Elle and Ron together were happy no matter what struggles they had to go through.

After putting Ron to bed, Elle laid down. The kids in the neighborhood were loud, but Elle had learned to cope with the madness and the noise out of necessity and she certainly didn't want to confront them. Elle knew as a single woman that it was not advisable for her to confront the rowdy teenagers. She quickly fell asleep for her daily two-hour nap in between jobs. Then, a loud ring woke her up. It was the phone. Elle took a moment to get her composure because she had only been asleep for about thirty minutes.

"Hello?" said Elle.

"Hey girl, it's Tasha."

"Hey Tasha."

"Elle, I'm sorry but my car broke down and I won't be able to make it to your house tonight."

Sounding very disappointed, Elle said, "Oh no, you're kidding? Can I come and pick you up?"

"No, sorry," said Tasha. "Elle, my car stopped way across town and it would probably take you too

long. Plus, I don't want to leave my car."

Defeated, Elle said, "Okay, well I have to hang up, I need to try to get another sitter."

"Okay bye," said Tasha with no remorse.

Still half asleep, Elle had to make a very difficult decision. Tasha had missed nights before and even though Elle had seven sisters, she knew none of them would come help her. Their relationship was strained at best and hostile at times. Elle knew it was virtually impossible to find someone to come watch her son at this time of night on a weekday. Elle pondered to herself, *Do I call my boss and tell him I can't come to work after he told me the last time I called off I would be fired if I missed another day, or do I leave little Ron home alone and pray he doesn't wake up and nothing bad happens?* The options were terrible, but Elle would be looking at homelessness if she lost one of her jobs. The pain from being evicted from a home as a child was still very fresh in her mind, so she made the very difficult decision to leave her son at home alone. She struggled with this but being a very spiritual lady and a child of God, she left Ron at home by himself expecting God would watch over him and everything would be okay. She prayed and cried all the way to work. Elle cried a lot. How did they get here? She went from a fairytale wedding with the love of her life to a divorce from a despicable man whom she now hated.

It all started when she was a child. She was the typical PK -

Preacher's Kid. She enjoyed wholesome activities like roller skating, going to movies, bowling and just hanging out with a large group of friends on a regular basis. The group of kids, which included girls and boys, would go out together and laugh, talk, fellowship and just enjoy life. As often happens in these situations, as the group got older, some of them became romantically involved: puppy love. It was nice as they coupled off and continued to hang out together. As years went on, one of the couples withstood the test of time and they continued to date into adulthood. Bert was a skinny kid who laughed all the time and was one of the clowns of the group. He was very active in the church and he was a wholesome, overall good guy. Elle was a beautiful girl who grew up in a house full of attitudinal women. She was smart and hardworking, and she even had a job in high school. With a preacher for a father, Elle was very involved in the church. Bert and Elle met at church. They were childhood friends, high school sweethearts, now engaged to be married. These are the stories that make for great and inspiring relationships when they work. The couple did everything right from a PK perspective. Preachers teach their children to abstain from sex until after marriage and Elle did not break this promise to her dad. The young couple also did not cohabitate prior to marriage. Therefore, the desire to take the relationship to the next level was there, and after all this time, it was the right time to get married. They were ready.

They began their path towards marriage by making arrangements for the wedding. Elle's uncle was thrilled to be selected to marry them at her father's church. They rented a hall for the reception, they ordered flowers, and secured a photographer. They meticulously prepared all the plans for the wedding. They even found an apartment where they would live after marriage.

For Bert, the selection of his groomsmen was easy. He simply chose his groomsmen from the group of kids he and Elle had fellowshipped with for years. For Elle, the selection process went differently. The conversation went like this: "Girl, all of my sisters want to be in the wedding, but they want me to pay for the dresses, and you know we don't get along that well." Elle carefully chose three of her sisters and added a few friends to eliminate some of the potential for conflict.

The ceremony was held in a beautiful ornate church with family and friends in attendance. The church was filled to capacity and the bride was as beautiful as ever. The groomsmen were nicely tailored and clean cut and the bridesmaids were lovely, even though Elle's youngest sister Bon, who had the nickname Bon, arrived in a slightly different dress. Bon's dress was the same color, but it was lower cut, it had a shorter hemline and it was tighter than the other dresses.

Before the wedding Elle looked at her in slight dismay and said, "Bon, where'd that dress come from?"

Bon replied, "I couldn't pay that much money for a dress and only be able to wear it once, so I made a few alterations so that I could wear it again."

Elle, trying to maintain her composure, replied, "Whatever."

Throughout the day, there were spats between sisters and the bride tried her best to maintain a positive attitude and maintain her glee. She was able to do this, because after all she was marrying the love of her life and nothing could sadden her on this day. The wedding party was stunning and the wedding ceremony was flawless.

After the ceremony, the wedding party went to a very beautiful botanical garden near the Art Museum. This is a very common destination for bridal parties in Cleveland. The couple took beautiful pictures to be shared in their wedding albums and they lit up the area with their bright all white wedding attire. Although Elle's sisters had bickered throughout the day, it was her friend Rhonda who complained the most about the heat. Rhonda continued asking, "How much longer do we have? It's too hot!" It was hot, but that's what happens when you have weddings in July. One of the highlights of the day was when Rhonda, who had complained about the heat while they were taking wedding pictures, fell in the pond. Everyone except Rhonda laughed; it was funny as hell. They retrieved Rhonda from the pond and the picture taking was done. Sometimes God has a sense of humor. Perhaps this was his way of cooling Rhonda off.

The reception followed the photoshoot and all the

ceremonial traditions were done. They cut the cake, threw the garter and the bridal bouquet, they had the first dance and then were off to a wonderful start of their new life together. She was the perfect bride: young, beautiful, a child of God. He was the glowing, honest young church-going fellow that most mothers would be proud to have as their son-in-law. They were the perfect couple. At the young age of twenty-five, they had embarked upon holy matrimony. They moved into a nice apartment, talked and planned for a wonderful life together and they lived the great life of newlyweds. They continued to fellowship with groups of friends and still went out together to movies and dinner to laugh and enjoy life.

And within a year, life stepped in. Bert, who worked as a laborer, made a modest living and Elle worked as a secretary. They lived in a city and a time where jobs weren't always secure, Bert lost his job he had held since he graduated from high school. The loss of Bert's job was not tragic however because the salary was not large enough to really hurt them, or so they thought. As a year went by, the young couple continued to survive with Bert working odd jobs and Elle at her same position as a secretary.

Then, the news came... they were going to have a baby. The couple was thrilled, though their financial means were meager. They lived a simple life and had no real cause for concern. Nine months later, the baby arrived. All was wonderful in the young couple's life. Then it happened.

Bert, who was only twenty-seven years old, became ill. He had what seemed to be a simple viral infection. Elle took care of Bert at home and for a few months. He was in and out of the hospital because the symptoms wouldn't go away. The illness initially didn't seem serious, but within a few months, Bert passed away.

Bert didn't have life insurance, which left Elle with only her income to sustain her and their son. Elle even had to obtain contributions from the church for his burial. In addition to not purchasing life insurance, another miscalculation the couple made was to rely on life insurance from Bert's job. In this situation, Bert had lost his job and because of that, he lost his life insurance. For years and years, this young widow who had never planned on being the head of household was forced to survive as a single parent.

Elle was an obedient child of God, so eventually her situation got better. She was able to land a position where her salary nearly doubled. Because of her increased income, Elle was told if she bought a house, she would be in a better financial position than paying rent. Purchasing a house at this time provided tax benefits, also being an owner and building wealth through homeownership is a positive move. Elle moved forward and purchased a house. Unfortunately, she purchased the house right before the housing bust of 2007 and 2008. The house was in a nice neighborhood, but it turned out to be a money trap. In a normal market, she would have been able to use the equity in the house to borrow from and make repairs. Because the housing market crashed, and she was "underwater," she couldn't make the repairs when they were required. There were many needed repairs and because of inspectors bearing down on her, she eventually let the house go into foreclosure.

Elle moved back into the apartment where she stayed prior to the foreclosure because it was affordable, and Ron knew some of the children in the neighborhood. Years had passed, and Ron entered school and became a latch-key child. Elle, who was still young and beautiful, had a social life that consisted of going to work, church, and spending time with Ron. Her friends always asked when she might start dating again, but this wasn't a focus for Elle. Certainly, she could use and enjoy love and companionship from an adult and some help around the house wouldn't hurt. Also, as a PK, she was always taught that God will send you a mate when you're ready. Then It happened. Elle was at choir practice and a young man named Ricky joined the choir. Elle had seen Ricky in church but hadn't ever had a conversation with him. In churches there are usually more women than men, and Elle's church was no different. The women in the church had been trying to get Ricky's attention but Elle had not participated in the chase.

As choir director, she introduced herself and Ricky said, "It's great to meet you, sister in Christ. I want to join the choir because I want to serve the Lord the best I can."

Ricky was a charming, articulate and well-dressed man. He

wore expensive cologne and always said the right thing. After a few encounters, Ricky made it clear that he was interested in Elle. Elle, who was in her thirties at the time, still hadn't had much experience in dating and relationships because her one and only love she had met as a child. Ricky was flashy and exciting, and Elle slowly got involved with him. It had been sometime since Elle had had a relationship with a man but she still believed in abstinence until marriage, so their desire for each other and what seemed like love led them to get married.

Elle was happy with the marriage, which was entered with a much simpler ceremony than the elaborate wedding her and Bert had. Because Elle met Ricky in the church, she believed he could be trusted. Wrong! Ricky was a con artist who preyed on innocent church women. There were tell-tale signs. The couple got married and he moved in with her. He got her to purchase two Cadillacs and upgrade her apartment because he always said, "My queen deserves the best," but his credit wasn't strong enough to allow him to make the purchases, not to mention the assets he said he had were in his mother's name. Ricky eventually left Elle, or more accurately, abandoned her and left her with extensive debt, tax problems, and a broken heart that was overshadowed by the disgust she now felt for her ex.

Key Steps for Increased Financial Empowerment:

1. Elle's life shows many of the tragic situations where women often find themselves. The initial action Elle and Bert should have taken at the onset of their marriage was to receive financial counseling. That would have identified the need for life insurance and the need to save. At the age of twenty-five, a good term life insurance policy for half a million dollars would have only cost them a about fifty dollars a month. As a young couple who planned to live together forever and have children, they should have purchased a policy and held on to it because insurance is the foundation of keeping a financial house in order. With insurance, once you pay the first premium payment on an approved policy, you are covered immediately for the entire insured amount, even if it's millions of dollars. When you're young, it's not always possible to save that much money as quickly. If Elle would have received half a million dollars at Bert's death, her financial life would have been much better.

2. Bert and Elle had low paying jobs and hadn't saved any money for emergencies. People don't often feel they can do this because their financial needs are not being met. If you can't pay your basic household expenses, how do you save? The reality is the situation may never change and if you are not prepared for an emergency, the results could

be dire. What should be done in these situations is the concept of paying *yourself* first. When I was young and living on my own after college, my mother would call me and ask, "How much money are you saving?"

I would always tell her, "Mom, I can't save any money because I don't make enough to cover my bills."

She'd then ask, "Did you go to the nightclub this week?"

Crickets! I had no response because I did take care of my social needs, so I just needed to slightly adjust my priorities to save some money. Saving NEEDS to be a priority. If Elle had savings when she bought the house, she may have been able to pay for the repairs.

The best practice for saving money is to set up an account where you can have money drafted out of your bank account at least once a month and deposited directly into another savings account you don't touch, except for emergencies. Ideally, the account would be a mutual fund or a brokerage account where you can invest and typically receive more income and interest than a basic savings account. It doesn't matter how small the amount; the key is to develop the habit. Be realistic! Even when we are struggling financially, we spend money on non-necessities. For instance, you could cut out buying coffee or lunch once a week or all together. If you buy a dollar cup of coffee every day, that's thirty dollars a month. If you go to Starbuck's and spend two dollars for a small cup of coffee, it will cost you approximately sixty dollars a month or seven hundred and twenty dollars a year. Can you make coffee at home for less? You can park a little further from the job and save on parking while improving your health. Take the bus instead of driving to work.

A ritual I follow at least once a year is to review all my bills and call the companies and ask for reductions. This includes cable television, cellphones, asking for lower credit card interest rates, you name it. I never go through this exercise and don't cut my cost.

Here's the typical conversation: "Hello, cellphone company?"

"Yes, sir?"

"I think my bill is too high, I just saw an ad on TV where you're offering four lines for fifty dollars each. I pay more than that."

"Okay sir, we appreciate you patronage. Let's see if we can help you out. Please hold."

A minute or so passes, then I hear, "Hello sir, sorry

for the wait. It looks like we have another package where we can offer you everything you currently have plus a few additional features for less. This is a special promotion for a year and after a year, the price will go back up."

Typical savings for this type of call is twenty-five to fifty dollars per month.

Over a year's time, that could be six hundred additional dollars to put towards your emergency savings. Do this with all your bills and you could easily save more than one hundred dollars per month. Also, get rid of those magazine subscriptions for magazines you don't read and any expense that doesn't provide value. Once the money is free, add it to your periodic savings amount or pay off debt. When you get a raise at work, always add a portion to your savings. As you solidify this habit, you can add more to the monthly amount as time and income progresses. Doing this will change your financial life.

3. The other issue is that of preparing for a new relationship. It's critical to know who you are sharing your life with. This is a very hard conversation to have but as seen here and throughout this book, the results of choosing the wrong life partner can be devastating. At the

higher income levels, a pre-nuptial agreement is a real answer. In today's world, it is not uncommon for women to pay alimony. If you have a substantially brighter future than your potential mate, you will want to protect yourself. At the lower income levels, a good financial advisor can at least make you aware of the signs that may have been overshadowed by your love for the person. For instance, is the person in good health? The answers to this would come out in the application and issuance of a life insurance policy, which we now know is critical. Does the person have good credit and a good driving history? The answer to this question will come out in the application for auto insurance. Many people don't know they check your credit for auto and homeowner's insurance and if your credit is bad, you could pay more or be denied.

Please understand when you get married, your credit history and positive driving history could adjust lower because you have become one entity as a couple. I know this from personal experience. Prior to marriage, I used to drive a lot of fast cars and consequently, I also had a lot of speeding tickets. When Connie and I got married, her auto insurance went up immediately because she was in the same house with me and they assumed I would have access to her car. Unless something terrible is revealed, taking these measures should improve the relationship and protect it from future shocks.

The good news from this story is Elle is fine now and her baby is a grown man with a job and a promising future. She still struggles financially, however, due to the debt and tax problems the ex-husband left her. She is still young enough in her fifties to hire a tax advisor to help her with her IRS debt and to engage a financial advisor now that she is an empty nester who only needs to take care of herself. She may be in a position to prepare for a better retirement. In addition to the other solutions, a comprehensive financial plan in the beginning prepared by a professional could have saved Elle much of this grief. At minimum, the planner would have recommended sufficient life insurance, which could have changed this story completely. Also, good financial advisors become like family and they can really help you weather life's storms.

Helen – The Mogul

Helen and her young daughters stood in front of her husband's casket. She was tall and beautiful, and she wore a black dress and the modest but expensive jewelry elegantly. Yet the black funeral hat and veil fit well but looked terribly out of place; she looked too young to be a widow at only 44 years old. Her daughters were equally as elegant and beautiful wept by her side. They were only teenagers. Lourdes, the oldest daughter, was weeks away from her prom and high school graduation. How could this be? How could it be this young woman, Helen, could be standing in front of her husband's casket. She was too young to be a widow.

Helen and her late husband Gary led a good life. They were pastors of a church and ran several successful businesses. They helped hundreds of people with their ministries and most importantly, they were obedient Christians. They walked a true Christian walk.

The funeral was painful, but in some circumstances, when there is long suffering, the death of a loved one can offer some relief.

It all started when Gary called me in November to file his taxes from the previous year. They had never been late in the past, but this year they filed an extension.

He told me, "Helen is in the hospital and this is why we're late."

I told him, "I'll come by your house and we can talk about moving forward."

When I arrived at the home, I was a little shocked. Gary had lost a significant amount of weight.

I said, "Hey man, how are you?"

> *"It's been a little rough lately because Helen had cancer. She is fine now and staying at her mom's house for recovery."*
>
> *"So, how have you been man?"*

"I've been a little under the weather. As you can see, I have lost a little weight."

"Yes, I noticed. What's going on?"

He told me, "Nothing much, I'm just a little tired. I haven't been sleeping much since Helen has been in the hospital."

We went on with the business of the day and ended our appointment within an hour. I followed up with Gary with the taxes within a week. All the past due taxes were complete.

"Gary, I'm done with your taxes and they are ready to be filed."

We then set a time to meet, which we did. He completed reviewing and signing the taxes.

I said, "It's time to do year end planning and preparation for next year."

"I know Mark, but can we just submit these and talk about this in a few weeks?"

"Absolutely, I'll give you a call in a few weeks."

Three weeks later, Helen was back home, and Gary was going for surgery. Yes, surgery.

Gary never spoke about his illness, but it was much more serious than I would have imagined. Gary had cancer. Neither Helen nor Gary seemed extremely worried since Helen had just had a cancerous tumor removed and seemed to be fine. They expected nothing less for Gary.

I told Gary, "I'll connect with you after the surgery to plan for next year."

Unfortunately, Gary had complications and as the months went by, Gary's health quickly deteriorated.

I had never seen anything like this. It appeared as if Gary aged twenty-years in only a few months. His hair had turned grey and his facial features looked like those of an old man. Gary was only forty-nine, but he looked to be in his seventies. This was very hard on Helen. Gary was her rock, the love of her life, her business partner, her gift from God. In addition to the challenges that were directly related to Gary's illness, Helen also had several businesses and a church to run. When you own your own business, you can't always take off like an employee on a job. Helen and Gary's income was dependent on their businesses. So, amid all that was going on, Helen still had to take business calls and take care of all their holdings.

Helen was up to the task because for as long as I have known Helen, she was an astute businessperson and a high roller. When I met her, she had designer glasses, designer clothes, gold jewelry, and a pocket full of money. She was fourteen! She wasn't a young lady from a wealthy family in some well-healed suburb. She was the daughter of blue-collar workers who lived in a blue-collar suburb. The reason she was so well dressed is because she had two jobs and bought what she wanted with her money.

She worked, maintained an active social life and still maintained solid grades. Therefore, her current challenge was in-line with her fast-paced lifestyle.

Helen got used to the challenges of taking care of her sick husband, her children, and all their business enterprises. She was operating very well even though she had to take a moment for a cry, which was totally understandable for her situation. Then, Gary passed away.

The young widow now had a monumental task in front of her. She was now the sole owner of a large enterprise she had run in the early years with her husband, but like I've seen several times before, when children are born, they become the focus and the business is left for the husband to manage. This works out fine, until it doesn't.

To get through the task of dealing with the estate, luckily, she had a great relationship with the financial advisor, me, and I was able to walk her through everything. She had a complex estate with properties and businesses needing to be retitled. She had assets and insurance policies to be claimed and retitled and equally important, assets needing to be protected from the next potential suitor. I have seen where the next man can come into the life of a vulnerable, grieving woman and wreak havoc, so if someone has assets, it is important to put things in order to protect the assets. When you're young, beautiful and rich, there are many suitors.

When you are getting remarried and have children, it is

important you pay attention to insurance policies, beneficiaries, and a will. Keep this in mind. If Helen remarried and she passed away, unless there was a will put in place, when the second husband dies, his kids would get all the assets that were accumulated by Helen and her first husband and Helen's children would get nothing.

Fortunately, the widow was in a good financial position.

Key Steps for Increased Financial Empowerment:

1. Helen had a complex estate with multiple companies and organizations of all types to manage. Helen was fortunate to have a great relationship with her financial advisor. If she didn't have the strong relationship, it would have been advised she meet with the advisor and determine if she felt comfortable with her. If not, she should have gotten a new advisor to take over or at least monitor the other advisor.

2. Helen has multiple entities to manage. She will need to decide of how she wants to proceed with the businesses. Does she want to sell them all? Sell a few? Have a management company or in-house employees run substantial pieces of the business?

3. Helen has a significant estate. She will need to consider how to protect her assets, whether it is a pre-nuptial agreement or complex corporate structures that will keep her assets safe. She should also prepare an Estate Plan her children will reap the benefits of all the wealth her and Gary built together.

.

CHAPTER 5

HEAD OF HOUSEHOLD

"Single moms, you are a doctor, a teacher, a nurse, a maid, a cook, a referee, a heroin, a provider, a defender, a protector, a true superwoman. Wear your cape proudly.' --Mandy Hale,
author

These are stories of the single moms. Single moms have extensive challenges, whether it's planning for the future, tax planning, shared custody of children, how to solidify insurance coverage, or how to structure their financial lives for success. Solutions are included for these complex situations.

Shelly – The "It" Factor

I had just arrived in my new city and I was on a mission to network and meet some good people. I was invited to a business mixer where I was introduced as the city's new CFO and gave the audience a brief introduction of myself. As the program continued, multiple speakers spoke and then the person with the "It" factor arrived. The lady had it all together. A red dress perfectly tailored for her, flowing, well-coiffed hair, excellent presence and a powerful, persuasive voice. Have you ever seen a person who knows how to work a room and brings a lot of energy? Shelly was it.

Shelly is the consummate professional. She is a corporate CEO, dynamic, and very popular in the community. She has held powerful positions in some of America's top corporations and she is a power networker. She has been able to mobilize large numbers of people for her designated causes and whenever there is something of note in the community, she is there.

After time had passed, I eventually reached out to Shelly to interview her for the book. I started with my typical leading question.

"Tell me about your experience with investments?"

Now to be fair, in some cases, I just informed the women I wanted to interview them for my book, with no indication of what the book was about. This was the case with Shelly.

She said, "To be honest, I am not where I need to be. I am a native of California and for many years, I had an illustrious career in banking. I performed the task of community banking where I worked on building the community with a human touch.

I replied with, "Having spent many years in banking, I was well aware of this position. In my town, it was the banker who was always pictured with a big check the bank was presenting to a business for expansion or to a community organization that did work to benefit the underprivileged.

She said, "Then, things changed. All of a sudden, the bank no longer wanted people with relationship skills; they wanted salespeople."

Again, I was familiar with this trend because I had colleagues who went through this as well.

With a lot of anguish, Shelly said, "Then they transferred me here. Well if it's not hard enough to make a lot of sales in your hometown, it's certainly hard to make sales in a totally *new* market. I had some good results, but I was not enjoying what I was doing and we eventually parted ways.

> *"Also, as you may know, I have two children, and it took a lot longer for me to find a job than I anticipated. Most of my retirement savings were used to sustain my family. I eventually got another job, but it was not at the level of pay I had become accustomed to."*

When we spoke, she had not invested and at this point, she was in her fifties. She clearly understood the need but due to her tight financial situation, she had not moved on investing. I discussed some of my findings from research that underscored the need to invest and she agreed with them all.

She said, "I am ready to make a move and I also want to assure my daughter, who is in her twenties, follows suit."

Shelly also affirmed the importance of my quest as she noted, "I could think of twenty women *immediately* who could benefit from the guidance you are offering."

She then said, "Where do I start?"

I informed her, "The first step is to analyze where you are."

She understood this is a big challenge for many people, to admit and face where they are. The truth is, this is essential. How can you plan to move forward if you don't know where you are? It's never too late to put yourself in a better position. At fifty, your income is typically as high as it has been and in Shelly's case, her children were grown and no longer totally dependent upon her. Also, at fifty, the government allows you to set aside larger amounts of money in retirement accounts in the event you are trying to catch-up.

Key Steps for Increased Financial Empowerment:

1. Shelly has had challenges like other people I have interviewed, and she is at an age where she may

feel like it is too late to get started. The reality is she needs to do a Financial Analysis to determine what her goals are and develop a plan to get there.

2. Retirement funds are needed as well as an emergency fund. Shelly needs to really understand and embrace the fact it is never too late to get started.

3. Shelly would like for her daughter to be better off than her. Shelly should start her on the right path and serve as a role model and guide on how to become more financially literate and financially independent.

Macadamia – The Entrepreneurs Daughter

Macadamia is another financial professional and having had several conversations with ladies who are financial professionals makes it clear it doesn't matter if you have an aversion to numbers or not. Investing is the black hole where there is not a lot of understanding. Guess what, it's intentional. There is a reason why everyone is not educated in investing. I'll leave that right here.

So, I started my conversation with Macadamia the same way as I had with others with some small talk and then I asked her, "Macadamia, what is your experience with or knowledge of investments?"

> *"Well Mark, I just purchased a new home and being close to fifty years old and I didn't believe my*

dream of building a home from the ground would ever come true, but it did. I am a single mother, so the dream of owning a home was intimidating."

"I understand Macadamia, I have rented apartments at times and there is nothing like having someone else having to worry about your repair woes, but home ownership definitely is a great move from an investment standpoint."

She said, "I planned well. I moved into to a one and one, which is a one bedroom, one bath apartment I downsized to in order to save for my home. I minimized my expenses and saved money. I saved money for five years until I had enough for a down payment and then I made my move."

I asked her, "where did you keep the money you saved for your home?"

"I kept it in in a standard savings account."

"Well Macadamia, for instances like this a standard savings account is not a terrible option. You may have been able to get a little more interest on your account if it were in a money market account, but the difference is not significant enough to squabble over.

So, what about your investments other than your home?"

She said, "I am invested in the retirement plans at work and I feel comfortable with that."

I asked her "how did you choose your investments?"

I talked to a friend at the time and they advised me how to allocate the funds into the investment."

"I understand Macadamia, this is not an uncommon occurrence. In the past prior to my becoming an investment professional, people would come to me for investment advice for their 401Ks.

Do you have any other investments?"

> *"I don't. A while ago had talked to my friend and we considered an investment advisor, but I didn't have enough money for that."*

I asked, "Do you understand you can invest in mutual funds for as little as $50 a month?"

> *"No, I wasn't aware of this. Also, I was not aware of where I could go to find such a person and that presented a barrier for me as well."*

Macadamia's primary understanding of an investment was investing in a home which is definitely a good move for her that has her very excited. Even though she just bought her first home, she is already planning to make another investment in five years following the same process she did for her current home.

I asked Macadamia, "who taught you about investing and she said "My father. My father had a very distinguished record as an entrepreneur and a real estate investor. When I was a child, we owned several businesses and my father had made many real estate transactions that increased our family wealth. My father helped with the purchase of the home, but he never showed me how to do things, he just did it. I am very proud of and love my dad dearly, but I would love to know some of the nuts and bolt of investing myself."

Of note, is Macadamia's frame of reference for investing is real estate. As was mentioned, her father who taught her investing was primarily someone who deals in real estate. My experience has shown me people who deal primarily in real estate sometimes only feel comfortable dealing with real estate. They are no different that the educators and finance people, they are comfortable with what they know.

"Macadamia, real estate until 2007, was a pretty easy investment to understand. You could expect if you bought a house as the years passed, the house would be more valuable, and you could sell it for a profit. This concept also applied to land. Real estate is tangible. You can go to a house you purchased and look at it, you can touch it. The stocks to some are not as tangible, although if you invest in Microsoft for instance, you can clearly see their products and you could go to many cities and you could see office buildings where they are located, but many people don't understand this correlation. When you buy stock, you are a part owner in a corporation.

I once convinced a friend who was a tax client and a real estate investor to invest in the stock market. After a few months he liquidated his positions and put that money back into real estate because that is what he was comfortable with. He had been a nurse who built a real estate portfolio worth a million dollars. This was pre-2007 before the housing crisis. The same portfolio was worth pennies on a dollar after the market tanked. So, the point here is although you and your father are more comfortable with real estate, it is always advisable to diversify your investments. "

The final conversation I had with Macadamia was about her relationships with a mate. "Macadamia you mentioned "your friend," my understanding of this term is this is a romantic relationship. Am I correct?"

She laughed and said, "Yes."

> "Ok, because we are friends, I want you to know now you have a substantial asset to protect, your home. You have to be very careful who you get involved with, especially if you were to get married. It is important they have good credit, otherwise he could hamper your ability to buy another home. You do know when you marry someone your credit history and other things like insurance are determined based on both of your lives, so if he has bad credit when you get married, you both have bad credit when purchasing jointly. I'll just give you an example, when Connie and I got married I had had a few speeding tickets on my record. Due to this Connie's auto insurance went up immediately when we were married. This is the type of impact marrying someone could have, so be careful. Can I ask, what do you desire in a mate?"

She noted," I am very spiritual and involved in my church, not only would the person have to be equally yoked, but he would have to be involved in the church, not just attend and pray. I do feel like having someone with good credit is desirable, but I don't feel like that was something that couldn't be repaired over time."

Knowing Macadamia as I do, it's clear one would have to be a quality person to be involved in her life.

Key Steps for Increased Financial Empowerment:

1. Macadamia is a very disciplined saver. She knows how to live within her means and plan. Macadamia planned the purchase of her home perfectly. She now needs to apply the same approach to her overall financial life, investments included. She needs to determine where she wants to be financially in retirement and what her other goals are, so she can plan to meet them like she did with the home purchase.

2. Macadamia is a new home owner. Macadamia needs to assure she has adequate insurance coverage on her home. She will also want to assure she has an emergency fund for potential home repairs.

3. Macadamia has expressed interest in purchasing another home for investments purposes. Macadamia should investigate some education in

what is involved in being a landlord. She also needs to understand the expenses related to a rental property to assure she is able to operate the rental property profitably.

4. Macadamia has not been trained in investing even though she has some investments, her retirement plan at work. Macadamia needs to seek out an advisor who can teach her about investments. Currently she is focused on real estate only. It would be worthwhile for her to understand other investments even if she decides to invest in real estate only.

5. Macadamia may get married in the future. Macadamia will want to make sure her assets are protected, and she will definitely need to have conversations about finances with her suitors before moving forward with marriage.

Jean – The Dearly Departed

Like in a popular sitcom from the nineties when fictional character Theo Huxtable would do

pushups, put on cologne, comb his non-existent mustache and put on his coolest clothes when his older sisters came home with some of their beautiful friends, I used to dream one of Jean's friends would want to fall in love with me. Younger brothers often try to appeal to their older sister's friends, yet with little luck. Jean wasn't my biological sister, but we were very close. Jean was that older sister of a friend who was good looking and kept company with all the pretty girls who ignored my friends and I completely because we were much younger. Jean was fun-loving and enjoyed every bit of life. As a friend of her brother, I spent a lot of time at her house and got to know her just like I did my own older sister. Anyone who had a sister who was a few years older can probably relate to the struggles young boys sometimes have with their sisters. As a young man, you try to act mature in your interactions with her friends, then she demands you leave the room. Your mother then follows up with, "Boy, go outside and play and leave those girls alone." Not the best way to attract an older woman. Even if one of the ladies were interested, sisters never let a relationship happen.

Jean grew up to be an attractive woman who loved to dress, in her own words, "slutty," because she enjoyed partying to the max and being provocative while doing it. As we grew older, the difference in age became less important and I started hanging out with her more than I did with her brother who went out of state for college. When we partied together, it was excessive. It usually involved my good friend who had just returned from the military and four or five of her friends. For many years, we partied hard and often.

Once we had both completed college my career progressed, and I became a financial advisor, I called Jean and scheduled an appointment to meet at her house. When I arrived, the house was immaculate. The house was a nice split-level home in the neighborhood where we grew up. She gave me a tour of the three-bedroom, two-bathroom house. The home was beautifully decorated in a style only she could have put together. Jean had embraced the Swahili culture. Her home was decorated with beautiful African prints and rugs. It was ornate with African Art and incense were burning to set a relaxing mood.

When we toured the home, I noticed she had two cars. One car was a small sports car and the other was an SUV. She also had a dog. It appeared Jean had it all together, but my experience told me she was probably living beyond her means and deep in debt. I came to that conclusion because it was an era when many young people were overextended with debt due to their need to maintain a certain lifestyle. Any good advisor pays attention to the unspoken in order to properly assess their client's financial situations.

After the tour, we sat down and laughed about old times.

She jokingly said, "So, you're selling insurance now?"

I laughed and replied, "No, I am helping people become debt-free and financially independent."

She said, "Okay, let's get this over with then."

As we talked, it was clear she was happy being single and she still lived "La Vida Loca" and loved it. Even though she worked, she enjoyed a very full social life full of clubbing and partying on her off days. She had no intention of settling down and was happy with her choices. She owned her home, her cars were paid for, she had cash in the bank and she had an investment portfolio other than a retirement plan from her job.

My dear friend who I partied with for years had turned the energy she previously used to party into work. She worked two jobs and managed her money well, which allowed her to continue to be a free spirit. Because I was a new advisor, I had no clear-cut reason to sell her life insurance. She didn't have children and she had cash in the bank to cover her burial, if needed. Because we were close friends and she wanted to help me, she purchased a small policy anyway and completed a financial plan and an additional investment account. Real friends help you out. After we finished doing business, we had some wine and laughed and reflected some more.

A few years later during my annual follow-up calls with clients, I called my dear friend and she wanted to meet. I heard she had a baby and I figured she wanted to set up a college savings account and purchase additional insurance. When I arrived at the house, Jean was using a walker. At the time, Jean was in her late thirties. She greeted me as always with an upbeat attitude and a smile. I tried my best to not look the way I felt inside, which was horrified. We began to talk and to my surprise, she was in good spirits and we had a gleeful conversation as usual. We began to discuss why she called.

Jean said, "Can you increase my life insurance policy? I have been diagnosed with a terminal disease and I'm not expected to live much longer."

I was devastated. The news hit me hard. This is someone I had known my entire life and we were just getting to the point in life where life was getting good because we were making good money and had a lot of options in our lives.

I told Jean, "The unfortunate thing about life insurance is it is like a bank loan. If you really need it bad, there is no way in hell you're going to get it."

Life insurance companies base their policies on the amount of risk being assumed.

Even if I could have sold her a policy, the price would had been too expensive for her to afford. Life insurance is typically only issued to healthy people or those who are not expected to die soon. To make the situation even more dire, her job was in a traditionally male-dominated profession, so she was fired from her main job upon pregnancy.

She said, "When I asked my boss for time off to have the baby, he said he didn't know what to do. They had never had a woman in the position before,"

So eventually, they fired her. She filed a discrimination suit, which she eventually won. I instructed Jean I would talk to some higher-ups in my company and determine how we could best help her.

As time passed, Jean continued to become more ill. With the loss of her main job, she had also lost her medical coverage. The assets she had so carefully accumulated had also become depleted. Because of the seriousness of her illness, she had to spend down assets to get Medicaid. Her primary medication, which included a device that pumped medicine into her, cost $150,000 per year. With no medical insurance, this was an impossible amount to sustain, so Medicaid was essential.

In addition to her medical issues, she was also concerned about her son. What would happen to him? She knew she was terminal and had to have hard conversations and make serious decisions. She had purchased a small life insurance policy but Jean's child, who was only one years old, might not have money to sustain him for life. She ultimately decided to grant her brother guardianship.

Jean was such a trooper and a good person, during her final days, she called me to her house to talk. She had a list of her friends and acquaintances who she called and told them they needed to talk to me about life insurance. This wasn't so that I could make money, it was out of concern that what happened to her could happen to them. It was touching but sad at the same time. We were able to get some people covered, but at minimum, we let them know what could happen.

Her son was very fortunate to have a support system that could sustain him after her untimely death. Jean's brother had significant resources to care for the child and his daycare and sitters remained the same, allowing the child to not endure additional trauma.

Key Steps for Increased Financial Empowerment:

1. Jean's son was a minor when she died and was not able to receive any funds until he was an adult. Having gone through this experience, it is important to note when purchasing life insurance, if it can be avoided, the beneficiary should not be a minor. In this case, the parent died when the beneficiary was a minor. The guardian had to go to court every time they wanted to access money; therefore, a thorough estate plan should be set in place to allow the flow of funds to be easier.

2. Jean's life changed dramatically. She went from a vibrant single woman with no responsibility to anyone to a mom with a terminal illness who left a child alone by her death. Life happens, and if you are not prepared financially, you could be devastated. Or in this case, leave your children potentially devastated. Due to the velocity of what happened with Jean, the solutions aren't always

clear, but to avoid some of the devastation, one should have their financial lives in order.

Fortunately for Jean, she had a lot in place and she didn't suffer through much financial devastation. Although she fared well through the storm, having disability insurance to cover her income once she became sick would have helped. A larger life insurance policy, a will and a living will would have been helpful also. In this scenario she was able to enunciate what she wanted to happen, which was Do Not Resuscitate, but having everything in order through a concise financial plan in advance helps extreme situations be less stressful.

Feria – The Millennial

Young people who are enjoying a carefree lifestyle are the hardest group to convince to focus on investing. When you're partying in exciting places like Miami, New York, and Dubai at a young age, saving money and planning may not be at the forefront of your thinking. Feria was no different. She was in her twenties and her career was moving fast. She runs a complex department and is well liked by all. She enjoys a very full social life. She never slows down between work, raising a daughter, socializing, and keeping fit at the gym. She was also known to be the life of the party.

One friend said, "I love her, but she's too generous when we go out, buying rounds of drinks for others and spending heavily."

Feria was very secure with her lifestyle.

When we started the discussion about her finances and investments, based on her friends' comment, I asked, "Do you have a budget?"

She said, "I have the B-Word, but I don't follow it."

Although she didn't feel like she was in a bad situation, she said,

"I have no focus on investments. I don't feel I should deprive myself by putting a large portion of my money out of commission by putting it into investments. I am a millennial and you know we are not interested in that type of stuff.

I'm into instant gratification and experiences and don't have a lot of interest in saving and planning for the future. I feel there are other types of investments that are important to me. I invest in myself and my career, which by the way, is going exceptionally well. I also invest in the top schools for my daughter, so she can have a secure future."

I told her, "Certainly, investing in yourself and your children are worthy and important, and the dividends could outpace any other investments."

Feria's job offers a deferred compensation pension plan which is mandatory and has a significant match. Beyond this, she does not participate in any other investments. I asked, "Why haven't you put any time into investing your money?"

> "Well, I know beyond stocks, real estate is supposed to be a good investment, but I have made a conscience decision not to purchase a home in order to be more flexible when it comes to my career. Also, in the back of my mind I always believed one day I would get married and a man would take care of me financially."

She then openly admitted, "I know this is not a great solution, especially for an independent woman like me, but it is my reality."

So, where do we go from here? I really appreciated Feria's honesty and openness. I also appreciate her opinions. The purpose of this book is to help people, even when they may feel like they don't need it. Feria will need to read the stories of the women who were once like her and understand they are saying, "I wish I had started when I was young." The great thing about this process is I have put the thought of investing into many minds. Several ladies have come back to me and reported they have restarted investments they had abandoned, or they investigated life insurance to protect their families. That's what this book is all about, to help women be more successful.

Key Steps for Increased Financial Empowerment:

1. Feria lives totally for the moment. She is young and believes it's the only way. Living for the moment is an excellent choice but ignoring there is a future is problematic. Feria has a child and even if she is fine living for the moment, she needs to assure a solid foundation is in place for her daughter. She needs to start by purchasing adequate life insurance and putting a will in place to assure in the event of her death, her money can easily flow to her daughter.

2. Feria has not begun to seriously invest and doesn't have many assets because she has decided not to purchase a home. The decision to not purchase a home is a smart one because she based it on her chosen lifestyle. She wants to be flexible to allow for career growth, wherever it may be. She should, however, start to accumulate some financial assets through investing so if she ever has a setback, she will have something to fall back on to sustain her until the situation improves. There are many women in this book and many others who I have encountered over the years who regret the fact they didn't invest when they were young and vibrant and had the energy to work harder and make a lot of money. Feria should seize the day.

Saving and investing shouldn't hamper a lifestyle, it should enhance it.

3. Feria has admitted she hopes a man will come into her life and handle the money to assure she is in good financial shape. Feria should take some time to learn about financial literacy through reading and attending a few seminars. She has free financial advisors available to her at her job. She should spend some time with them. If she does find the man who will come in and take care of her, it'll then be a bonus. What if she doesn't, or worse, what if she finds a man like Keith, from the story about Bernie, who can't manage money either?

Anna Rose – Parent Extraordinaire

I met Anna Rose about two years ago at a financial conference and I was extremely impressed by her abilities. I believe I am one of the top financial professionals in the world, but Anna Rose, who is much younger and has a lot less experience than I, was able to figure out computer challenges much quicker and with more finesse. Anna Rose had a job and a few side hustles to make additional money, so I thought she would be an excellent person to interview for this book.

I met Anna at a healthy restaurant. Before we met, I asked her, "Where would you like to go for lunch?" to which she responded, "Somewhere where I can get a salad."

Anna is very health conscious and is an excellent athlete.

"Anna, I believe I've told you about the book I am writing?"

"No Mark, you didn't."

I was a little surprised I hadn't told her. I divulged the whole story about how the idea originated with a conversation with my sister.

"Wow Mark, that's a great story!"

"Anna, I started this book many years ago, back in 2009. Do you want to know what really got me moving?"

"I do," she said very inquisitively.

"Well, it was two events. First, I had started this book after the conversation with my sister, but many years later, I had almost the same conversation I had with my sister, with her

daughter. The other event was when I arrived in Palm Beach, I met with a lady to interview her about the book and she said, 'Mark, you're writing a book? That sounds great! What page are you on?' I responded with what I am sure was a very silly look on my face, 'Do you mean in my mind or actual physically written pages?' We both laughed, but for me, it was a real call to action. Who was I kidding? It was time to get busy, and here I am!"

"Okay, so Mark, what page are you on now?"

"Anna, I am just about done. I am submitting the book to the editor for a final review this week."

"That's amazing, I can't wait to read it!"

"So, Anna, tell me about your experience in investing."

"Well as you know, I have two children of my own and I adopted two more. You also know I am a single mom."

"Yes, I recall you telling me that."

I was so impressed with Anna when she told me she had two small children but had a calling to adopt two older children who were less likely to find a permanent home. *What single woman does that?* Anna is very well grounded, and it is quite apparent she really loves all her children.

"Well, there was a time when I thought investing would be a great thing to learn so I tried to learn it, but I got distracted and quit. My boyfriend helps me now."

"Okay, do you have any investments?"

"Other than the retirement plan at work, no."

"Okay, so how did you choose the investments in your retirement plan at work?"

"You mean I had to choose investments? It was such a blur. On the first day of a new job, they give you a bunch of information and everything was just so confusing. I never did meet with the lady who was supposed to counsel us..."

"Well, I believe what they do nowadays is put your money in a fixed investment or a target date fund as a default. The fixed fund is like a bank account with a fixed guaranteed rate of return. The target date fund is based on your age, so since you are twenty-five, they would give you a fund with a horizon of about forty years. The fund will start off

with aggressive investment because you have a long way to go and when you get closer to retirement, the investments will be conservative, so you won't lose any of your money when you are close to retirement."

"Well, now I am going to check with our advisor at work and find out what I really have. I could be losing money!"

I informed Anna that she was not alone; many women have the same issue. I identified this in the book and offered further guidance.

"You did? You identified this problem in other women?"

"Yes, the book starts with some stories of multiple women, not just the rich and famous, but everyday women who need advice. I found one of the biggest reasons people struggle is their lack of understanding of how money works. I use the stories, so women can hopefully identify with one or more and understand how to make their own situations better. I then go into explaining common terms that typically confuse people. I conclude with showing you how to invest, step-by-step, including things like how to setup a brokerage account."

"It's amazing you said that. I opened a brokerage account and really didn't know what to do, so I closed it eventually. What happens if you only have a little money in the account? Do you have to buy like five shares or something?"

"You could buy a few shares, or you could just let your money accumulate until you are ready to make a purchase."

"Wow, I didn't know you could do that."

"Yes, the brokerage will keep your money in a money market account until you decide to make investments. They will give you interest on your account and when you are ready to invest, you just send in or call in the instructions and your money will be invested."

"Do you explain all of this in your book?"

"It's in there, yes. I met with my niece this weekend and she asked me several questions, and for each one, my continued response was, 'It's in the book!'"

"So, you explain how stocks work?"

"Yes, that is also included."

"You explain how to choose stocks?"

"Yes, that information is also provided."

"Can I lose all of my money, Mark?"

"Yes, but you being a financial guru need to understand this: When you buy a stock, you are buying a small piece of a company. If the company you chose is solid, such as if they have a solid financial record, strong sales, and good products or services like Google and Amazon, the chances of losing all your money is less likely; however, for someone like you I would suggest you invest in mutual funds, initially. Do you know what a mutual fund is?"

"Yes."

"Okay, what is it?"

And with a big smile, Anna said, "Okay, maybe I don't know what a mutual fund is. Do you explain this in your book?"

"Yes, it is included. A mutual fund is a pooled investment, so just like when you buy a share of stock, you own a small piece of a company. When you buy a mutual fund, you own a small share of

many companies. So, if you had a mutual fund with Enron, when Enron collapsed and became worthless, in your mutual fund you would have many other companies in the fund keeping your money stabilized. Mutual funds diversify your money, so the likelihood of all of the companies going under is less likely."

"Wow, this is really great information! I can't wait to read your finished book!"

Key Steps for Increased Financial Empowerment:

1. Anna has an investment at her job, but she doesn't know how it works or where her money is. Anna should go to the consultant at her job and have her give a thorough explanation of the plan, the investment options, and where she is to date. The consultant can also do a suitability test to determine what investments are best for Anna.

2. Anna doesn't have a focused plan, nor does she know where here financial life is headed. Anna needs to have a Financial Analysis prepared so her financial life can be more focused, and it can be determined if she has critical needs, like life insurance and an emergency fund.

CHAPTER 6

JUST THE FACTS MA'AM

"In investing, what is comfortable is rarely profitable." -- Robert Arnott

I have talked about the WHYS and we've seen some of the stories underscoring *why* to invest. As I continue this journey to discuss women and investing, it is important I touch on some of the facts related directly to effective money management and investing. I'll start with the numbers explaining why women tend to have less in investments and why it is crucial to have more. Most of us already know women live longer than men.

I often joke, "That's because they kill us!"

Back to the facts, a study conducted by UBS Wealth Management seem to support this claim. They suggest women in the USA live 6.7 years longer than men on average. Living longer means women will face higher expenses over a lifetime versus men. They will have to meet their necessities for more years and because they live longer, they will have to pay other costs like healthcare and medicine expenses, which will continue to increase as they age. In addition to living longer, women tend to work a lower number of years. One of the primary reason's women work less is because they are more likely than men to take off time to care for children. According to the same UBS study, "Men work 38 years over their lifetime, while women work just 29 years." If the first two statistic above aren't enough to convince you, studies also show women earn just eighty-three cents on the dollar compared to men.

Therefore, if you combine longer lives with higher expenses, lower wages, and shorter work lives, it underscores why women need to invest more and to be knowledgeable about investing to maximize the amount of money they have.

Women openly admit they have less investment experience and knowledge than men. In a Wells Fargo study, 60% of men reported they were extremely experienced in investing compared to only 42% of women who had the same level of confidence. Even with this admitted disparity, other facts show the women who invest often fare better than their male counterparts.

According to data from financial services giant Fidelity

Investments, women are superior investors. By reviewing more than 8 million investment accounts, Fidelity discovered women not only save more than men, .4%, their investments earn more annually, also .4%.

According to Alexandra Taussig, Fidelity's Senior Vice President, "The myth that men are better investors is just that - a myth." The study noted although the percentage of difference is small, if you started with a 22-year-old earning $50,000 per year, a woman investor would outpace her male counterpart by more than $250,000 by retirement age. Even with this information, when asked what gender the better investors are, barely 9% said it was women.

There is psychological research suggesting men are more likely to be overconfident about finances than women. I must admit this no surprise to me; I have dealt with hundreds of families and the men almost always claim to know more about investing.

There are various reasons why women who invest are more successful. In the Wells Fargo study, it was determined women's actual investment behavior tends to follow recommended investment practices more often than men. The study found single women traded 27% less frequently than single men, possibly because men tend to be overconfident about their investment ability. Psychological studies show overconfident investors tend to trade more, which results in higher direct and indirect costs. The study also showed women tended to have a more disciplined approach to investing than men. For example, online investment company Betterment, found male investors invest 100% of their accounts in stocks at least *twice* as often as women.

The practice of having all money in stock doesn't represent diversification, which is a best practice in investing. Men are also six times more likely to make massive allocation shifts, switching from 100% stocks to 100% bonds or vice versa. This final fact could explain the others: Women are more likely to seek education and advice from investment professionals. In another Wells Fargo survey in 2014, twice as many women compared to men indicated what they need most from the advisor is education about investing principals and concepts.

I have often told my sons to "invest in what you and your friends buy the most." Since they are millennials, the purchases they typically make are most likely trendy. I also tell them to invest in solid industries like food.

This approach also applies to helping women make good investment decisions. Women make 70% of household purchases, putting them in a great position to benefit from a strategy once made famous by Peter Lynch, the best-known mutual fund manager on the planet. Lynch, who ran the famous Fidelity Magellan Fund from 1977 to 1990, said in his book *One Up on Wall Street*, "Investors research tools are their own eyes and ears; he got some of his best investment information while walking around shopping malls and talking with his friends and family."

Do you need more compelling reasons why you should handle your money well? Here's more: 9 out of 10 women will eventually take charge of their family's wealth. 40% of women are their family's primary bread winner, 45% of the millionaires in the United States are women, and women control $14 trillion of personal wealth in the United States. How about them apples.

The Information Gathering Process

Social media a wonderful tool for research. Due to my many years as an advisor, when I set out to write this book, I felt I had enough stories and information to write a comprehensive book about women and investing. To be as thorough as possible, I embarked on additional research. I ventured out to social media and asked standard questions to hundreds of women. The questions are as follows below:

What challenges do you have with money? For example, some of the answers I have already received are:

6. Help with debt
7. Understanding investments
8. My 401K
9. Keeping up with bills
10. Challenges being a single mom
11. Choosing a financial advisor: Is it the taxman, insurance agent, other

The questions were based on some of the issues brought to me most often as a financial advisor.

Debt

What are the best methods to pay off debt? You may ask why we are talking about debt in a book about investments. First and foremost, although the primary focus of this book *is* investing, overall money management is a component of investing. Debt is a four-letter word your mother hopefully told you about.

Debt has crippled many people, rich and poor. The process of pushing people into debt is like how drug dealers get people addicted to their products. They start off by making access easy, free offers at low or no cost. They let you use a little and as soon as you begin to use a little more, they raise your limit a little more. Before you know it, you have gotten into more debt than you can pay off monthly. Then amazingly, another card comes in the mail which allows you to go a little further, and the process repeats.

Many people use credit as a part time job. What I mean is if they don't have enough money, they supplement their income by charging items. Just like most money challenges, debt is not restricted to those who don't have education or money.

I will never forget when I counseled a couple who had annual income of approximately $250,000, back when this was an obscene amount of money. The couple, who were in their thirties, had no children. They both had good jobs, the wife made $200,000 and the husband made $50,000 annually. That same income would be approximately $370,000 nowadays. They wanted counseling because they wanted to purchase a new home. The challenge was although they had extraordinary salaries, they had racked up a boatload of debt. The debt included a wedding they spent $30,000 on *plus* $10,000 for the honeymoon. She wore a $15,000 ring they charged. They had two Mercedes and the accompanying car notes. They had an additional $45,000 in miscellaneous credit card debt and student loans totaling more than $100,000. Their total debt was in excess of $400,000, and remember, they don't even have a house yet. Shocking? Absolutely.

So why would they do this? Many people initiate debt with the premise they could stop and pay it off at any time if they wanted. Sound familiar? Such as the addicts' mindset. There is no difference.

Okay, so debt is not a good thing. But what if they still had enough money to save for a home? They were both in the retirement plans at their jobs, but should they start building an investment portfolio outside of their retirement plans? What do you think? I say **NO!** The first thing they should do is to begin to pay off their debt because the interest they were paying was a large amount.

If you have credit card debt, let's say something low like $1,000, compare interest payments you are paying on the debt to what the same $1,000 would pay you in interest in a bank account. Clearly, a bank account is rarely the best investment, so take the current return of the S&P 500, which is a well-known stock index to gauge market returns and apply it to the $1,000 and make the same comparison. Most likely, you would still be better off paying off the debt and experiencing the, "Oh, what a feeling it is to be debt free!"

Credit

Credit goes hand-in-hand with debt. If you have or have had debt, you have a credit history. If you paid your debts on-time, your history will be good. If you didn't pay your debts on-time, your credit history will be bad. Whether or not your credit is good or bad will be reflected in your credit score or credit rating; these terms are synonymous. You should really think about your credit score as an asset or a liability, and here's why:

If you have a good credit score, which is 700 or more, you will be able to buy houses, cars and receive loans somewhat effortlessly; if you have sufficient income to pay back the loans. If you have poor credit, you may not be able to purchase any of the aforementioned items. If you are able to purchase them, you will have to pay very high interest rates, which will translate into much higher payments. Something many people don't understand about credit is many jobs check your credit before they will hire you. When employers check your background, many look at your credit, especially if you are like me and work in a financial profession. The other industry checking your credit is insurance companies. When you apply for auto insurance, for instance, the companies check your credit. If you have poor credit, this could result in a denial for insurance or high rates. Remember the definition of an asset is something of value. For this reason, I would consider a good credit score as an intangible asset and if it is negative, it is a liability.

Understanding Investments

Do you understand investments? was the next question. Most respondents stated they didn't understand investments. The most frequent reference was to the 401K plans. For many of the women, the 401K plan was their only exposure to the stock market. Luckily many of them had begun to invest at least a minimum amount, even though they did not totally understand them. Their questions were mostly on what they were supposed to invest in. The great thing about 401K plans is they are relatively simple. The employer takes money out of your paycheck before taxes and they may match some of your contributions. When a deduction is made before taxes, the amount deducted has a lower impact on your take-home pay For instance, a $50 deduction might only lower your take-home pay by $40.The money is typically invested in mutual funds and the better plans offer a good selection of mutual funds, but not too many to keep the plans manageable. There are literally thousands of mutual funds, so companies limit the number offered to avoid overwhelming employees. They provide statements on a regular basis and many of the providers offer services such as counselling and advising. To simplify the process even more, most plans now offer mutual funds based on your age or your investment horizon. The funds are called age based, or target date funds. These funds use your age as a guide. For instance, if you're thirty years old, you could invest in a thirty-five-year target date fund which will take you to the retirement age of sixty-five. The funds mirror what an advisor might suggest. The funds start off aggressive and as a person gets older, they begin to invest in more conservative investments to maintain the current level of money. When you are about five years before your retirement, your portfolio will be almost 100% in fixed and very safe investments.

Understanding 401K investments, which was a primary question asked, is just a small part of investing. You have stocks, bonds, unit investment trusts, mutual funds, annuities, and even though most don't always think about this, insurances should always be a part of investment plans. Other than retirement plans at work, most respondents didn't have separate portfolios. At best, some had a mutual fund account. There is a lot more to investing, much of which will continue to be discussed throughout this book. The world of investing is vast, so the understanding may not be easy, but with some effort, you will develop a solid approach.

Understanding the 401K Plan

When asked about investing in 401K plans specifically, the answers were overwhelmingly that women may not understand them. Again, this is not an issue exclusive to women, but the interviews identified it as a prevalent issue. The typical scenario for retirement plans is that you get a brief presentation and they provide you with a book and a bunch of investment options. They next tell you to bring it back completed.

Many people have come to me throughout my career and asked, *what do I do? What should I invest in?* My advice is as follows: Yes, you *should* invest, and you should invest the maximum amount the employer matches. Otherwise, it's like giving away free money. Taking advantage of the company match is an investment which is providing you with a 100% return!

To conclude 401K's, I will inform you that one woman mentioned she felt many women don't ask questions about these issues because they are embarrassed to show they don't understand. She asked me if this is a women-only issue. It is not.

The chapter on "Types of Investments" will offer more information on the investments available for 401K plans.

Managing Expenses

What are strategies to lower your bills? Another issue was that of paying bills. I have already talked about debt, which is a separate issue from bills. You can be debt free, but still have bills. When I talk about a bill, I am referring to regular expenses, like gas for your car, bus fare, utility bills, electricity, water, insurances, rent, taxes, and groceries. We all have expenses we must pay to maintain our lifestyles. Bills can be more challenging than debt because many of the bills we pay never go away. Even if you sell your car and no longer require purchasing gas, it may be replaced with having to pay bus fare or Uber expenses.

The best way to handle bills is to develop a budget, which is another essential component of money management. Effective budgeting will allow you to have a spending plan. If you spend without a plan, you may not make the best use of your money. The budget will help you maximize your money. There are many strategies that can be used to lower your regular expenses, which will be discussed in the "Get Started" section later in the book.

Amazingly, I received hundreds of responses to my social media survey. The respondents ranged from women who came from impoverished backgrounds and were single mothers to PhDs, mayors, media personalities and some who grew up with the silver spoon. Given the social media survey questions above, there was rarely anyone who couldn't identify with one of the issues.

I did have one woman who said, "I date an NFL player; I don't have money problems."

Outside of her, most of the respondents had some challenges.

One of the most prevalent issues I must say I was unaware of was the number of women who had started their own businesses and failed. This made keeping up with debt and bills very challenging. Many stated the business failures were due to lack of knowledge on how to grow their businesses. Some had business tax challenges and one I recall was an investigative reporter who mentioned the strain of legal challenges she faced from being an aggressive reporter. She noted she never lost legal battles, but they were costly and severely affected her profits.

Another similar and related issue was job loss. Some of the research was done in a down economy and many people, not just women, had lost their jobs. Like those who had business challenges, many of the women had spent some time unemployed. Part of being unemployed or having business failure was the usage of 401K money and other savings until they were completely depleted. I have to say during my many years as a tax preparer and CPA, I always thought if Congress wanted to help people out, they would eliminate the penalties on early withdrawals of retirement accounts and the 7.5% threshold before medical deductions are allowed.

When these women withdrew 401K money due to a layoff before age 59 1/2, they were subject to a 10% penalty and the withdrawn money being added to their taxable income; therefore, costing them a lot of money. For example, if someone withdraws $20,000, the penalty would be $2,000 and the additional taxes could be an additional $3,000 at the 15% tax rate. This scenario played out over and over with the women I interviewed. The problems with job and business stability are not exclusive to women, but I must say, I was surprised how prevalent it was in the female population.

I was very impressed with the large number of women I spoke to who had ventured out into entrepreneurship. I have personally done a significant amount of business with women-owned companies, including all facets of this book like the cover, editor, translator, website, etc., and they always do a great job. Part of the reason some women-owned businesses may fail is access to capital. Studies show women on average asked for $35,000 *less* in business financing than men. They get approved for debt financing at a lower rate than men, and women get approved for business loans less often than men. They also receive lower amounts. With those statistics, it is no wonder women have struggled. We must fix this because the more successful women-owned businesses are, the more successful the overall economy will be.

Another challenge was the issue of single parent homes. Many of the women were single parents. Some had significant incomes, but many were challenged with maintaining a home on their own and consequently, they didn't feel they had time nor the proper resources to learn about investing.

Financial Advisors

Based on the previous section, the natural next question is, if you don't understand investing, why not get a financial advisor? Crickets, I say! That's right, when I ask this question in person, the typical response is nothing, a mere blank stare. The odd thing about our society and money is most of us spend a lot of time attempting to make money, but most people don't spend a lot of time trying to find out what to do with it once they get it.

Congratulations to you! If you are reading this book, you have made the conscious effort in deciding to take a step in the right direction and learn about money. Hooray!

The reasons why the respondents hadn't selected an advisor were varied, but the primary reason was they didn't know who to trust. Talking to people about money is not always easy. Having been a CPA for many years, I understand if you are knowledgeable in where money is spent, you have considerable insight into someone's life; therefore, you must be someone who can be trusted with some of people's deepest secrets. I have mastered this and to be a great advisor, confidentiality is a must!

What I found equally as odd is there are some people who don't want to work with their relatives. Perhaps they don't feel their secrets are safe? Even the well-known and famous financial advisor Suze Orman, realized some of her very closest friends were not in good financial shape and they did not come to her.

In her book *Women and Money: Owning the Power to Control Your Destiny,* she stated, "Upon further investigation, I had learned that so many women in my life, friends, acquaintances, readers, people from my TV audience, all had this obstacle in common: an 'unknown factor' that prevented them from doing the right thing with their money. It doesn't matter if I'm in a room full of business executives or stay-at-home moms, I find the core problem to be universal: When it comes to making decisions with money, you refuse to own your power, to act in your best interest. It is not a question of intelligence. You absolutely have what it takes to understand what you should be doing. But you simply won't bring yourself to take care of yourself financially, especially if those actions compete with taking care of those you love. Your inner nurturer reigns supreme; you do for everyone before you do for yourself."

CHAPTER 7

TALK THE TALK AND KNOW THE RULES

"You have to learn the rules of the game and then you have to play better than anyone else."--Albert Einstein

This chapter presents investment terms that are sometimes difficult for those not in a financial profession to understand. A barrier to investing I have noticed is the terminology used for investments. I became a CPA prior to embarking on a career as an investment professional and many of the terms and concepts were very familiar to me. There were many new concepts and theories, but I think my financial background indeed helped; however, I too encountered challenges. I say this, so it is understood there is a knowledge gap existing for us all. If you work with an advisor, don't be too intimidated to ask for a definition and explanation of the terms and jargon she uses. I know for a fact some financial professionals try to dazzle you with their "brilliance" instead of assuring you understand what they are talking about.

This brings me to the topic of financial education. One of the problems with financial education is that most schools who take the time to educate children in financial literacy often bring in bankers. I'm not going to go on my normal tirade about bankers, but miseducation is quite often the result of what it is they do. It may not be malicious; it's for their business advantage.

They talk to children about opening savings and checking accounts. They may even talk to them about debt, but please understand and acknowledge it is *not* in their best interest to educate children about investing. Banks take your money and invest it into the market. They give you very low rates of return while they reap the much larger returns from investing in the stock market. They make their money lending *your* money to others. They may not pass any of their gains on to their customers.

On the flip side, when the Federal Reserve raises interest rates, the banks almost immediately pass those additional costs on to you. Banks do very little to truly help their regular customers be in a better place. However, if you have millions of dollars, you will receive much better treatment from bankers.

I am sharing this because there is no reason for banks to thoroughly educate you about investments. Banks typically talk about passbook savings, CDs, credit cards, and annuities. These products are very profitable for the banks, so this is where they focus their discussions.

Here's an example. Years ago, I went to a bank and made a pretty significant deposit and the teller asked me if I would like to open an annuity. At the time, I was in my twenties or thirties. **Please understand you cannot withdraw your**

money from an annuity without a penalty from the IRS and the bank until you are 59 ½ years old! Therefore, my money would have been locked up and unless I paid the bank's heavy penalties, I wouldn't be able to access my funds for thirty years.

I asked the teller, "Why did you make that recommendation?"

He said, "No one has ever asked that question..."

Why would the teller do that? My experience tells me annuities pay large commissions to those who sell them. Annuities are not bad products; it is a great product when the time is right, but there was no effort on the bank's part to understand my needs.

So now, let me educate you on some financial terms to make you more successful with your financial endeavors. I'll talk about some of the terms you probably hear the most and the rest are in the glossary located in the back of the book.

I asked my wife Connie what words she hears most, to which she replied, "Stock market, Dow Jones, mutual funds, IRAs, and what's that other one...?"

I said, "Annuities? Roth?"

"That's it, Roth! Then I hear pre-tax, and from that point, I hear Charlie Brown's teacher saying, *womp, womp, womp, womp, womp.*"

Let's start with stock market, also known as "the market." The **stock market** is where investors buy and sell shares of stock in public companies. The stock market and stock exchange are basically the same thing. When you hear someone talking about the **New York Stock Exchange (NYSE)**, they are just talking about one of the many markets or exchanges where you can buy and sell stocks, also known as trading. Now let's talk about the **Dow Jones** or **Dow Jones Industrial Average (DJIA)**. It is an average of thirty significant company stocks traded on the NYSE and Nasdaq, which is another market. The DJIA is simply a tool to gauge how stocks are performing on a given day. If you hear the Dow is up, there is a good possibility your investments in stock are up also and vice versa if the Dow is down.

Now I'll talk about stocks and mutual funds. When you buy a **stock**, you are buying a small piece of a company, also known as a share. If for instance you bought shares in Enron, which at one time in history was a great company, when they went out of business, you would have lost all your money. However, when they were making money, you would have shared in the profits. Now I'll compare a mutual fund to shares of stocks. A **mutual fund** is a pool of money collected from many investors for the purpose of investing in securities, which are typically stocks and bonds. Unlike a stock where you can lose all your money if one stock goes bad, a mutual fund has many stocks or bonds included, so like in the previous example, if Enron goes out of business, you still have other stocks in your mutual fund keeping your money positive and diversified. Mutual funds are a good investment for those who are learning how to invest.

On a side note, while I am writing this section, I have determined looking up investment terms is probably not user-friendly for most people. Just like I am writing this section and seeing the need to define words in the definitions, looking up investment terms works the same way. So, let me go back and define a few terms I just used. I'll start with securities. A *security* is a certificate or other financial instrument that has monetary value and can be traded. Stocks, bonds, and mutual funds are all types of securities. *Traded* refers to being bought or sold.

The other term I used is diversification. *Diversification* means you are spreading your investment dollars over more than just one investment. Here's another term: liquidity. *Liquidity* refers to the ability to transfer hard assets to cash. For instance, if you own a home or investment property, it is not very "liquid" because for you to turn it into cash, you must sell the home, which could take a while. Mutual funds on the other hand are somewhat liquid because you can cash them out and get cash in a week's time. The most liquid investments are those that are in cash, like savings accounts and money market accounts. You can receive your cash from these investments immediately.

Here is another term you may hear: *Initial Public Offering, or IPO*. An IPO is when a company converts from a private company to one which its stock is sold in the market, also known as public companies. Here is an example of an IPO. Imagine you own a company that makes clothing. The company was started by your parents and since you took over the company, it has begun to grow quickly. Due to the explosive growth, you expand your operations to provide clothing to stores in multiple locations. Your company continues to grow, and you decide you want to make your company a global enterprise, but you don't have the money to achieve this goal. You talk to your accountant and he suggests you turn your privately-owned company into a public company, meaning you allow others to invest in your company by purchasing stock. The investors purchase stock, which provides you with money to expand your business. Now, people other than your family are part owners of your company. Your company is no longer privately-owned; it is a publicly owned company. Because this is the first time you have offered people outside of your family to invest in your company, it is an initial public offering, as noted earlier in the definition. The process of an IPO is complex, but this example gives you a baseline explanation of what an IPO entails.

IPOs are exciting because they are ground floor opportunities to invest in a company before it grows substantially. For instance, if you would have bought a thousand shares of Google, now known as Alphabet at $85 per share, $85,000, you would have made $1,065,000 because at the date of writing this book, the stock is selling at $1,250 per share. Don't get too excited though because there are obstacles to be able to participate in an IPO. You typically need to have at least $100,000 in cash or liquid assets and you must have traded several times in the past year. Like the old saying goes: "You have to have money to make money."

The final term is margin, or you may hear someone bought *stock* on margin. **Buying on margin** means you have borrowed money to buy securities from your broker. This is where people get into trouble. Let's say someone bought one thousand shares of stock at $100/share, thus spending $100,000. Now let's say that stock price dropped to $10/share. The investor would have experienced a $90,000 loss, which the broker who lent the money will be requiring payment on almost immediately. If you can't pay, the broker will most likely take legal action against you to recover their money.

This just scratches the surface on terms. Some other terms you should be familiar with are money market accounts, term life insurance, interest bearing checking accounts, exchange traded funds (ETFs), and annuities. Please refer to the glossary I have provided for your easy reference in the back of the book and you can also look up terms on Investopedia. And please, if an investment professional uses a term you are not familiar with, **ask them what it means**!

CHAPTER 8

TYPES OF INVESTMENTS

"An investment in knowledge pays the best interest."--Benjamin Franklin

I've discussed obstacles and questions surrounding money management and investing. Now it is time to discuss the actual investments. Before I get into the different investments, I think it is essential I clarify one major source of confusion. The issue is the difference between an investment and an investment vehicle or account. There have been many times when I have recommended a mutual fund to a client and they ask if they could also get a Roth IRA. I explain the mutual fund could be the investment in the Roth IRA account. Unlike a mutual fund, a Roth IRA is not a type of investment. A Roth IRA is a type of account. You can hold investments such as stocks, bds, cash, and, yes, even mutual funds, within a Roth IRA. This applies to 401K plans and traditional IRAs, which again represent the account type or investment vehicle holding the investment. Now I have explained the difference between an investment and an investment account, now let's discuss *types* of investments.

Think of the various types of investments as tools that can help you achieve your financial goals. Each broad investment type from bank products to stocks and bonds has its own general set of features, risk factors and ways in which investors can use them. I will start with a discussion on stocks and bonds, which are the most discussed investments. Stocks represent ownership in a company. When you own a stock, you own a small piece of the company. When you hear that Warren Buffet or Richard Branson own companies, what that means is they own most of the stock for the company. Others could own a lot of shares but don't own the majority. For instance, Facebook has 2.9 billion shares outstanding, of which Mark Zuckerberg, the CEO, owns about 28% at the time of this writing. Just like any business owner, stockholders can make huge gains, lose all their investments, or fall somewhere in the middle.

Bonds on the other hand, are considered debt, not ownership. When an investor purchases a bond, they are loaning money to the organization. Stock owners get dividends if the company decides to share a portion of the profits. Bonds, however, pay interest payments on the amount of the bond, which as I mentioned, is a loan. The interest payments are typically paid every six months and at the end of the bond's term, the investor gets the principal, which is the amount loaned, back. If an investor keeps a bond for the entire period, they won't lose any money, unless the company cannot pay. If the investor sells the bond, they could lose money if interest rates currently available have increased to be higher than the bond, making it less valuable.

Because stocks and bonds are different, one being company ownership and the other being debt, they have what is called an inverse relationship. Simply stated, this means when stock prices are going up, bond prices are going down. It is often recommended your investment portfolio includes both stocks and bonds so when one is not doing well, the other which should be doing well can be an offset guarding against losses.

Having more than one type of investment is called diversification. Stock ownership can be volatile because if the company goes out of business, the stock is worthless. In the same vein, when a company goes out of business, they are required to pay off their debtors before any property or assets can be distributed to stockholders, so bondholders have a leg-up on stockholders in a business liquidation. Since bonds are typically safer than stocks, bonds typically have lower investment returns.

Stocks

Stocks come in a wide variety and are often described based on the company's size, type, performance during market cycles and potential for short and long-term growth. Let's start by talking about stocks classified by size. Here are three categories: large cap, mid cap, and small cap. This category refers to (cap)italization, which is the amount of money invested into the company. Small caps are companies with capitalization of less than $2 million like Rockwell Medical and First Internet. Mid-caps are $2 - $10 million like Dycom Industries and Steris. Large caps are $10 million and above like Amazon and Google.

You may also hear large caps called blue chips. They are the largest and most financially strong companies. I would guess you haven't heard of the small cap companies and may not have heard about the mid-caps, but certainly you've heard of the large caps.

Defensive versus Cyclical

Now let's talk about defensive versus cyclical stocks. Defensive stock companies sell products and services people need regardless of the overall economy. Groceries and pharmaceutical drugs are examples of defensive products. No matter how good or bad the economy is, people must eat and take their medicine. Cyclical stocks are the opposite. They are stocks of companies affected by the overall economy. Typically, luxury items and travel fit into this category. When times are hard, people are less likely to spend a lot on travel and extravagant items. When investing, you want to consider which type of investment yours is, so you can know what to expect in differing types of economies.

Growth, Value, and Income

You will hear investments discussed as growth, which represents a company expanding its operations and becoming more valuable. Growth stocks can be in any category of capitalization, but they are typically mid and large caps. Many of the companies in this category are in technology or industries prone to growing larger and more valuable. Value stocks are just that, stocks being sold at prices lower than would be expected based on factors like the company's financial strength. They are sometimes referred to as undervalued stock, which is a fitting description. Income stocks are those providing income in the form of dividends, which is a portion of profits shared with people who own stock in the company.

So why would you choose one over the other? The reason for choosing growth and value stocks is similar. When you by these types of stocks you are expecting the company will grow stronger and increase your investment. The difference is when you buy a value stock, it will be lower priced; therefore, your return on investment should be stronger. The good thing about experiencing growth in your investment is you don't have to pay taxes on the growth unless you cash out the investment. For instance, according to Investopedia, if you would have invested $100 in Amazon in 1997, your investment would now be worth about $120,000, representing a lot of growth in your investment. If you haven't cashed out the stock, you don't have to pay any taxes on the $119,900 gain. Now if you had received the $119,900 gain in dividends or by selling the stock, you would have had to pay taxes on the gain. Although this book won't touch heavily on taxes, smart tax strategies are important in money management and investing.

Penny and Speculative Stocks

You will hear people talk about Penny Stocks. The stocks in this category don't really cost a penny; however, they are normally under five dollars per share. There are penny stocks that do well but due to their size, it takes much longer to make a significant amount of money. For instance, I bought 300 shares of a stock in a well-known company for $4 per share. The stock is now worth $6 per share, which is a 150% gain, which as a percentage is very impressive. But from a monetary standpoint, it is only a $600 gain. This is more than my bank account would have paid, but it is not a lot of money.

In a similar category, as Penny Stocks are Speculative Stocks. Speculative stocks are stocks with a high degree of risk, such as a penny stock or emerging market stocks. Emerging market stocks are those in countries not as well developed as the US, like Egypt or Iran. Anytime you invest in industries in these types of countries, it is a speculative, high-risk investment. The benefit of speculative investments is with high-risk, there can be higher returns. The downside is it is easier to lose all your money.

<u>Bonds</u>

I talked about bonds earlier to differentiate them from stocks. In this section, I will give a more thorough explanation. A bond is a loan an investor makes to an organization in exchange for interest payments over a specified term plus repayment of principal at the bond's maturity date. There are many issuers of bonds and many different types. Corporations issue bonds, which are sometimes called Corporate paper. Governments also sell bonds. When a city, county, or state sell bonds, they are called municipal or muny bonds. The interest you earn on most muny bonds is tax free.

The federal government also issues bonds. You will hear them called several names including treasuries, agencies, bullets, and T-Bills, which are notes (loans) which have shorter payback periods but act the same as bonds. Treasuries are bonds sold by the United States Treasury, hence the name. Agencies are sold by agencies of the United States, like the Federal National Mortgage Association, better known as Fannie Mae. Treasuries are backed by the full faith and credit of the United States, while the agencies are not. Even though the US does not fully back agencies, they are still relatively solid and safe investments.

The other bonds you are probably familiar with are savings bonds. Many of you may have had these as children or you may have purchased some for your children. Unlike the US bonds we have already discussed, savings bonds don't pay interest in the same way. With these bonds, you pay an amount less than the total value of the bond and at the end of the period, you get the full-face value of the bond. I recall as a child, my mother would have me use $5 of my allowance every other week to buy a US Savings Bond, which at maturity would be worth $25. Since the savings bonds don't pay interest payments, they are called zero-coupon bonds. Coupon is a term used to refer to the interest rate on a bond.

As I mentioned earlier, unlike more speculative

investments, bonds purchased from financially strong organizations will always pay back your principal and represent a solid investment.

Mutual Funds and Exchange Traded Funds (ETFs)

I talked about diversification earlier in the book and I must reiterate diversification in investments is a *good* thing. The old saying of "Don't put all your eggs in one basket" is relevant in investing. The challenge is most of us don't have time or the expertise to comb through investment journals and business publications to determine which stocks and bonds to invest in. For that reason, the investment professionals on Wall Street developed investments funds.

Funds—such as mutual funds, closed-end funds and exchange-traded funds—pool money from many investors and invest it according to a specific investment strategy. There are hundreds of strategies, some of which I talked about earlier like growth and value. You can also buy funds focusing on a specific industry or investments from a specific country or region. An investment professional can help you decipher the many different strategies, or you can do your own research. Funds can offer diversification, professional management and a wide variety of investment strategies and styles. Understand the difference between stocks or bonds and a mutual fund, when you buy a stock in a company like Ford or a bond from the US, you are buying one entity, Ford or the US. When you buy a mutual fund, which could consist of all stocks, all bonds, or a mixture of both, you are purchasing many stocks or bonds simultaneously whenever you make a purchase. For instance, when you buy one share of a mutual fund, it could include a very small piece of ownership in one hundred companies. Therefore, mutual funds give you immediate diversification. But not all funds are the same. Understand how they work, and research fund fees and expenses.

Above, I talked about a closed-end fund. This is a mutual fund where there is a limited number of shares available. Once those shares are sold, then the fund is closed and no one else can purchase them unless they buy them on the secondary market from someone who owns shares. The other type of mutual fund is an open-end fund, which means there is an unlimited number of shares sold.

The other type of investment funds is Exchange Traded Funds, also known as ETFs. ETFs are relatively new on the horizon of investments. The first ETF in the US was 1993. ETFs hold assets such as stocks, bonds, commodities, and some hold mutual funds. An ETF is an investment fund traded on stock exchanges, much like stocks and they trade throughout the day at a price based on what investors think the market value is. ETFs often have lower fees than mutual funds and they typically have lower expense ratios. For the past several years I have been guiding people and companies to ETFs, but a lot of investment advisors don't like them because they have lower fees, which translates into lower commissions.

Bank Products

Banks and credit unions can provide a safe and convenient way to accumulate savings and some banks offer services that can help you manage your money. The typical products offered by the banks, other than checking and savings accounts, are Certificates of Deposits (CDs) and Money Market accounts. CDs are investments for a certain period, like six months, a year, or up to around five years. CDs offer higher interest rates than typical savings accounts because your money is locked-up for the designated amount of time and there are penalties for taking your money out before the period ends.

Money Market accounts are checking accounts with higher interest rates than a typical checking account. The reason for the higher interest is because Money Markey accounts normally have higher cash requirements. It typically requires you deposit at least $500 and you must maintain the minimum balance to not incur fees. If you meet the minimum balance requirements, Money Market accounts offer liquidity and flexibility. In comparison to stocks and bonds, bank products are guaranteed. When an investment is guaranteed, the return on investment is typically lower than those without guarantees.

I must add a caveat here. When I mention a guarantee, I am referring to what happens in normal times. In catastrophic scenarios when there are bank failures and other irregularities in the market, the guarantees may not apply or may be limited.

Bank products like Money Market accounts are best used for emergency funds. Unless you are very conservative and risk averse, you don't want to put large amounts of money in the bank, unless of course we go back to the double-digit interest rates of the eighties. In 1983, there were CDs paying 13% guaranteed. That is a good investment. But typically, you keep your emergency fund in a bank product and invest the rest in higher yielding investments to maximize your money.

Options

Options can be made to sound easy and perhaps purchasing them is simple, but you need to have a good understanding of how the stock market moves in order to be successful. I will discuss options briefly but caution you to seek greater understanding before investing a lot of money in options. There are two types of options I will discuss: Calls and Puts.

Call Options

A call is the option to buy an underlying stock at a predetermined price (the strike price) by a predetermined date (the expiry date). The buyer of a call has the right to buy shares at the strike price until expiry. The seller of the call (also known as the call "writer") is the one with the obligation. If the call buyer decides to buy, also known as exercising the option, the call writer is obliged to sell her shares to the call buyer at the strike price.

Here's an example: I buy a call option to buy shares of a company whose shares are currently selling at $10/share for $15/share. The company experiences great growth and now the stock is selling at $25/share. Because of my option, I buy 10,000 shares at $15/share or $150,000 in total for the purchase. I could immediately sell these shares for $25 each or a total of $250,000 and immediately make a profit of $100,000. Understand a buyer of a call expects the stock price to go up and they want to place themselves in a position to buy the stock, but not at a price that is too high.

Put Option -A put is the option to sell the underlying stock at a predetermined strike price until a fixed expiry date. The put buyer has the right to sell shares at the strike price, and if she decides to sell, the put writer is obliged to buy at that price. People who buy puts expect the stock price may go down, so they buy a put in order to insulate themselves from losses.

Let's look at a similar scenario from before. Here's the example: I buy a put option to sell shares of a company whose shares I purchased at $15/share for $10/share. The company experiences great losses and now the stock is selling at $5/share. Because of my option, I sell 10,000 shares at $10/share or $100,000 in total for the sell. I could protect myself from losing the additional $5/share, which is $50,000.

Why use options?

A call buyer seeks to make a profit when the price of the

underlying shares rises. The call price will rise as the shares do. The call writer is making the opposite bet, hoping for the stock price to decline or, at the very least, rise less than the amount received for selling the call in the first place.

The put buyer profits when the underlying stock price falls. A put increases in value as the underlying stock decreases in value. Conversely, put writers are hoping for the option to expire with the stock price above the strike price, or at least for the stock to decline an amount less than what they have been paid to sell the put.

We'll note here relatively few options expire and see shares change hands. Options are, after all, tradable securities. As circumstances change, investors can lock in their profits (or losses) by buying (or selling) an opposite option contract to their original action.

Calls and puts, alone, or combined with each other, or even with positions in the underlying stock, can provide various levels of leverage or protection to a portfolio.

- Option users can profit in bull, bear, or flat markets.
- Options can act as insurance to protect gains in a stock that looks shaky.
- They can be used to generate steady income from an underlying portfolio of blue-chip stocks.
- Or they can be employed to double or triple your money almost overnight.

Steady income comes at the cost of limiting the prospective upside of your investment. Seeking a quick double or treble has the accompanying risk of wiping out your investment in its entirety.

Options aren't terribly difficult to understand. Calls are the right to buy, and puts are the right to sell. For every buyer of an option, there's a corresponding seller. Different option users may be employing different strategies, or perhaps they're flat-out gambling. But you probably don't really care, all you're interested in is how to use them appropriately in your own portfolio.

Options although being understandable, learning to use them to profit heavily is a skill less tenured investors don't possess. Hedge Funds use options, so if they were so easy to use, Hedge Fund gurus wouldn't be the only ones making huge gains. I wanted to discuss this investment in the book, but there could be another book on the usage of options on its own.

Annuities

An annuity is a contract between you and an insurance company, in which the company promises to make periodic payments, either starting immediately, called an immediate annuity, or at some future time, a deferred annuity. Annuities are the vehicle, like I discussed with Roth IRAs. An annuity allows you to invest money, typically into a mutual fund like investment. Annuities can provide income for the rest of your life.

I will discuss the deferred annuity first. A deferred annuity is similar and could be used by a company to fund a pension plan. The way a deferred annuity works is you put periodic, typically monthly payments, into an investment for several years. When the time period has ended, you get an amount paid out to you, which is also typically monthly, guaranteed for as long as you live. To give you an example, I have an annuity where I accumulated $150,000. The Insurance company has promised me a monthly payment of $1,300/ month for life once I turn sixty-five years old.

An immediate annuity acts like a deferred annuity on the back end, but there is no accumulation phase. With an immediate annuity, I could deposit on payment of $150,000 when I am sixty-five years old and immediately begin to receive the guaranteed monthly payments. What makes annuities so powerful is the guarantee of lifetime income. At $1,300 per month, once I live beyond about ten years I have won because I would have exceeded the $150,000, I contributed. If I lived to be eighty-five, the company would pay me an $156,000 over the amount I initially invested. On the flip side, if I die at the age sixty-six, the insurance company has won because they only had to payout about $15,600 of my $150,000 and they keep the rest.

The example I used where the insurance company keeps your money is based on what is called a life annuity. A life annuity is based on one life. When that person dies, the payments end. There are other options where the annuity can be based on two lives, like a husband and wife. This is called a joint annuity. If I use a similar example to that above where I deposited $150,000 and got $1,300/month in a joint annuity, I would get a lower payment of about $1,000/month, but upon my death, my wife would receive a monthly payment for the rest of her life.

There are other options you can use for the payout of annuities where you get payments guaranteed for a certain number of years and if you don't live long, your family will get the remainder of how much the payments would have been. These are called period certain. As I mentioned, annuities are sometimes used for retirement plans and in many retirement plans you get to choose how you get paid out. You can choose to get a lump sum, life payments to you alone, a joint payout, or a period certain.

You may remember the very sad story of the nurse whose husband chose the wrong payout option and left her destitute because he did not understand the impact of the payout decision he made. Please keep this in mind when thinking of annuities.

Retirement Accounts

In my opinion, the best retirement plan is a pension. There are only a few organizations that still offer pensions, mostly governmental agencies. A pension is a retirement plan where the company contributes money to an account for you, and you may be required to contribute as well.

Once you retire, the pension plan will pay you a set amount of income for the rest of your life. In a government I worked in many years ago, if I had stayed long enough to get a full pension, I would be able to receive 66% of what the average of my highest three years of annual salary was. 66% percent may sound low, but when you retire in most cases there are no children to take care of, there is no or a low mortgage, and expenses like clothing are much lower. Therefore, 66% could be a very livable amount of money.

There also numerous other types of investment vehicles that come into play when saving for retirement and managing income once you retire. The primary retirement savings plans are 401Ks, 403Bs, 401As, 457s, and on and on. The names for retirement plans are all numbers because they are related to a section in the Internal Revenue Code. Most of these plans work in similar ways. Your employer contributes a percentage of your income and you are required or may be given an option to contribute also. These plans are typically called defined contribution plans and unlike pensions, they don't always offer lifetime income. The other challenge is some of these plans are voluntary. That means if you don't participate, when it is time for you to retire, there is nothing there. Sadly, we are coming to an era where most people don't have pensions and it may be too late when they will realize there is nothing there for retirement. Social Security probably won't be adequate and many people will be in bad financial situations when they are not in the best physical condition to work.

The good feature all these plans have is the money is tax deferred, which means when you invest money in these retirement plans, all your earnings are not taxed until you take the money out at retirement. The other benefit is the money withheld from your pay is also tax deferred meaning you pay no tax on it until later in life when you take the money out.

There is a plethora of other retirement vehicles that can be used outside of your job to save for retirement also. The most popular are Individual Retirement Accounts better known as IRAs. A traditional IRA has features like the retirement plans offered by an employer. The contributions you make to your IRA are tax deferred and so are the gains on your investments. There is another type of IRA, which is called a Roth IRA. Unlike a traditional IRA, the money you deposit into the Roth IRA has already been taxed. The great thing about the Roth IRA, however, is the gains on your investment are not taxable, and when you take your money out at retirement, it is not taxed either. Over the years, I have seen where people take money from traditional retirement plans and suffer a hardship because of the amount of taxes they must pay. For this reason, a Roth IRA is a great addition for retirement planning.

In this book, I have talked about a lot of women who are entrepreneurs who own companies of their own. I won't go into detail, but there are also a lot of retirement plans that can be used in your business. Some of the plans are very easy and inexpensive to run and there are also plans where you as a business owner can benefit greatly for your retirement. Some of the plans for smaller businesses include the Savings Incentive Match Plan for Employees also known as a Simple plan, the Simplified Employee Pension Plan, also known as a SEP IRA, and a solo 401(k) to name a few. As a small business owner, you want to investigate these plans early for your own retirement and as a benefit for your employees, which will make your company more attractive to the best employees.

Saving for College

Like retirement plans, there are a lot of college savings plans, including 529 College Savings Plans and Coverdell Education Savings Accounts. College savings plans are discussed more in the next chapter.

Alternative and Complex Products

These products include notes with principal protection and high-yield bonds that have lower credit ratings and higher risk of default than traditional investments but offer more attractive rates of return. Learn more about their features, risks and potential advantages before investing.

Initial Coin Offerings (ICO) and Cryptocurrencies

These are speculative investments that come with significant uncertainty and many risks. Before you consider an investment in ICOs or cryptocurrencies. These investments are very risky and not really regulated, so I would suggest you do extensive research before investing in them.

Commodity Futures

Commodity futures contracts are agreements to buy or sell a specific quantity of a commodity at a specified price on a date in the future. Commodities include metals, oil, grains and animal products, as well as financial instruments and currencies. With limited exceptions, trading in futures contracts must be executed on the floor of a commodity exchange.

Insurance

Life insurance products come in various forms, including term life, whole life and universal life policies. There also are variations on these—variable life insurance and variable universal life—which are considered securities. Insurance policies are discussed more in chapter ten.

CHAPTER 9

EVALUATING INVESTMENT PERFORMANCE

"Beware of investment activity that produces applause; the great moves are usually greeted by yawns."--Warren Buffett on how the market can price things wrong."

Choosing investments is just the beginning of your work as an investor. As time goes by, you'll need to monitor the performance of these investments to see how they are working together in your portfolio to help you progress toward your goals. Generally speaking, progress means that your portfolio value is steadily increasing, even though one or more of your investments may have lost value.

If your investments are not showing any gains or your account value is slipping, you'll have to determine why, and decide on your next move. In addition, because investment markets change all the time, you'll want to be alert to opportunities to improve your portfolio's performance, perhaps by diversifying into a different sector of the economy or allocating part of your portfolio to international investments. To free up money to make these new purchases, you may want to sell individual investments that have not performed well, while not abandoning the asset allocation you've selected as appropriate.

How Are My Investments Doing?

Now, having discussed the various types of investments, it is important you understand how to evaluate how your investments are performing. In order to be as transparent and none subjective as possible, I have taken the information on evaluating the performance directly from the Financial Industry Regulatory Authority (FINRA).

To assess how well your investments are doing, you'll need to consider several different ways of measuring performance. The measures you choose will depend on the information you're looking for and the types of investments you own. For example, if you have a stock that you hope to sell in the short term at a profit, you may be most interested in whether its market price is going up, has started to slide, or seems to have reached a plateau. On the other hand, if you're a buy-and-hold investor more concerned about the stock's value 15 or 20 years in the future, you're likely to be more interested in whether it has a pattern of earnings growth and seems to be well positioned for future expansion.

In contrast, if you're a conservative investor or you're approaching retirement, you may be primarily interested in the income your investments provide. You may want to examine the interest rate your bonds and certificates of deposit (CDs) are paying in relation to current market rates and evaluate the yield from stock and mutual funds you bought for the income they provide. Of course, if market rates are down, you may be disappointed with your reinvestment opportunities as your existing bonds mature. You might even be tempted to buy investments with a lower rating in expectation of getting a potentially higher return. In this case, you want to use a performance measure that assesses the risk you take to get the results you want.

In measuring investment performance, you want to be sure to avoid comparing apples to oranges. Finding and applying the right evaluation standards for your investments is important. If you don't, you might end up drawing the wrong conclusions. For example, there's little reason to compare yield from a growth mutual fund with yield from a Treasury bond, since they don't fulfill the same role in your portfolio. Instead, you want to measure performance for a growth fund by the standards of other growth investments, such as a growth mutual fund index or an appropriate market index. Here are some concepts to consider when evaluating the performance of your investments including yield, rate of return and capital gains and losses.

Yield

Yield is typically expressed as a percentage. It is a measure of the income an investment pays during a specific period, typically a year, divided by the investment's price. All bonds have yields, as do dividend-paying stocks, most mutual funds, and bank accounts including CDs.

- **Yields on Bonds:** When you buy a bond at issue, its yield is the same as its interest rate or coupon rate. The rate is figured by dividing the yearly interest payments by the par value, usually $1,000. So, if you're collecting $50 in interest on a $1,000 bond, the yield is 5 percent. However, bonds you buy after issue in the secondary market have a yield different from the stated coupon rate because the price you pay is different from the par value. Bond yields go up and down depending on the credit rating of the issuer, the interest rate environment and general market demand for bonds. The yield for a bond based on its price in the secondary market is known as the bond's current yield. For more information on bond yields, see Bond Yield and Return.

- **Yields on Stocks:** For stocks, yield is calculated by dividing the year's dividend by the stock's market price. You can find that information online, in the financial pages of your newspaper and in your brokerage statement. Of course, if a stock doesn't pay a dividend, it has no yield. But if part of your reason for investing is to achieve a combination of growth and income, you may have deliberately chosen stocks that provided a yield at least as good as the market average. However, if you're buying a stock for its dividend yield, one thing to be aware of is the percentage of earnings that the issuing company is paying to its shareholders. Sometimes stocks with the highest yield have been issued by companies that may be trying to keep up a good face despite financial setbacks. Sooner or later, though, if a company doesn't rebound, it may have to cut the dividend, reducing the yield. The share price may suffer as well. Also remember that dividends paid out by the company are funds that the company is not using to reinvest in its businesses.

- **Yields on CDs:** If your assets are in conventional CDs, figuring your yield is easy. Your bank or other financial services firm will provide not only the interest rate the CD pays, but its annual percentage yield (APY). In most cases, that rate remains fixed for the CD's term.

Rate of Return

Your investment return is all of the money you make or lose on an investment. To find your **total return**, generally considered the most accurate measure of return, you add the change in value—up or down—from the time you purchased the investment to all of the income you collected from that investment in interest or dividends. To find **percent return**, you divide the change in value plus income by the amount you invested.

Here's the formula for that calculation:

(Change in value + Income) ÷ Investment amount = Percent return

For example, suppose you invested $2,000 to buy 100 shares of a stock at $20 a share. While you own it, the price increases to $25 a share and the company pays a total of $120 in dividends. To find your total return, you'd add the $500 increase in value to the $120 in dividends, and to find percent return you divide by $2,000, for a result of 31 percent.

That number by itself doesn't give you the whole picture, though. Since you hold investments for different periods of time, the best way to compare their performance is by looking at their annualized percent return.

For example, you had a $620 total return on a $2,000 investment over three years. So, your total return is 31 percent. Your annualized return is 9.42 percent. This is derived by doing the following calculation: $(1+.31)^{(1/3)} - 1 = 9.42$ percent. The standard formula for computing annualized return is $AR = (1+return)^{1/years} - 1$.

If the price of the stock drops during the period you own it, and you have a loss instead of a profit, you do the calculation the same way, but your return may be negative if income from the investment hasn't offset the loss in value.

Remember that you don't have to sell the investment to calculate your return. In fact, figuring return may be one of the factors in deciding whether to keep a stock in your portfolio or trade it in for one that seems likely to provide a stronger performance.

In the case of bonds, if you're planning to hold a bond until maturity you can calculate your total return by adding the bond income you'll receive during the term to the principal that will be paid back at maturity. If you sell the bond before maturity, in figuring your return you'll need to take into account the interest you've been paid plus the amount you receive from the sale of the bond, as well as the price you paid to purchase it.

Helpful Tips

Whatever type of securities you hold, here are some tips to help you evaluate and monitor investment performance:

- **Don't forget to factor in transaction fees.** To be sure your calculation is accurate, it's important to include the transaction fees you pay when you buy your investments. If you're calculating return on actual gains or losses after selling the investment, you should also subtract the fees you paid when you sold.

- **Review and understand your account statements.** In addition to fees, your account statement—specifically the Account Summary section—offers a high-level picture of your account performance from the end point of the previous statement, including the total value of your account. For more information, read FINRA's Investor Alert, It Pays to Understand Your Brokerage Account Statements and Trade Confirmations.

- **Calculate total return.** If you reinvest your earnings to buy additional shares, as is often the case with a mutual fund and is always the case with a stock dividend reinvestment plan, calculating total return is more complicated. That's one reason to use the total return figures that mutual fund companies provide for each of their funds over various time periods, even if the calculation is not exactly the same result you'd find if you did the math yourself. One reason it might differ is that the fund calculates total return on an annual basis. If you made a major purchase in May, just before a major market decline, or sold just before a market rally, your result for the year might be less than the fund's annual total return.

- **Consider the role of taxes on performance.** Computing after-tax returns is important. For example, interest income from some federal or municipal bonds may be tax-exempt. In this case, you might earn a lower rate of interest, but your return could actually be greater than the return on taxable bonds paying a higher interest rate. It's especially important to figure after-tax returns in taxable accounts. This is often helpful to do with a tax professional. You may find that the gains made in a taxable account are not as robust as you thought, leading you to consider other investments for your taxable accounts (for instance investments that appreciate in value, but don't pay income that can itself be taxed).

- **Factor in inflation:** With investments you hold for a long time, inflation may play a big role in calculating your return. Inflation means your money loses value over time. It's the reason that a dollar in 1950 could buy a lot more than a dollar in 2015. The calculation of return that takes inflation into account is called **real return**. You'll also see inflation-adjusted dollars called **real dollars**. To get real return, you subtract the rate of inflation from your percentage return. In a year in which your investments returned 10 percent, but inflation sent prices rising three percent, your real return would be only seven percent.

As you gain experience as an investor, you can learn a lot by comparing your returns over several years to see when different investments had strong returns and when the returns were weaker. Among other things, year-by-year returns can help you see how your various investments behaved in different market environments. This can also be a factor in what you decide to do next.

However, unless you have an extremely short-term investment strategy or one of your investments is extremely time sensitive, it's generally a good idea to make investment decisions with a view to their long-term impact on your portfolio rather than in response to ups and downs in the markets.

Capital Gains and Losses

Investments are also known as **capital assets**. If you make money by selling one of your capital assets for a higher price than you paid to buy it, you have a **capital gain**. In contrast, if you lose money on the sale, you have a **capital loss**. Capital gains and losses may be a major factor in your portfolio performance, especially if you are an active investor who buys and sells frequently.

In general, capital gains are taxable, unless you sell the assets in a tax-free or tax-deferred account. But the rate at which the tax is calculated depends on how long you hold the asset before selling it.

Profits you make by selling an asset you've held for over a year are considered **long-term capital gains** and are taxed at a lower rate than your ordinary income. However, **short-term gains** from selling assets you've held for less than a year don't enjoy this special tax treatment, so they're taxed at the same rate as your ordinary income. That's one reason you may want to postpone taking gains, when possible, until they qualify as long-term gains.

With some investments, such as stocks you own outright, you can determine when to buy and sell. You will owe taxes only on any capital gains you actually realize— meaning you've sold the investment for a profit. And even then you may be able to offset these gains if you sold other investments at a loss. With other investments, capital gains can become more complicated.

Mutual funds, for example, are different from stocks and bonds when it comes to capital gains. As with a stock or a bond, you will have to pay either short- or long-term capital gains taxes if you sell your shares in the fund for a profit. But even if you hold your shares and do not sell, you will also have to pay your share of taxes each year on the fund's overall capital gains. Each time the managers of a mutual fund sell securities within the fund, there's the potential for a taxable capital gain (or loss). If the fund has gains that cannot be offset by losses, then the fund must, by law, distribute those gains to its shareholders.

If a fund has a lot of taxable short-term gains, your return is reduced, which is something to keep in mind in evaluating investment performance. You can look at a mutual fund's turnover ratio, which you can find in a mutual fund's prospectus, to give you an idea of whether the fund might generate a lot of short-term gains. The turnover ratio tells you the percentage of a mutual fund's portfolio that is replaced through sales and purchases during a given time period—usually a year.

Unrealized gains and losses—sometimes called paper

gains and losses—are the result of changes in the market price of your investments while you hold them but before you sell them. Suppose, for example, the price of a stock you hold in your portfolio increases. If you don't sell the stock at the new higher price, your profit is unrealized because if the price falls later, the gain is lost. Only when you sell the investment is the gain realized—in other words, it becomes actual profit.

This is not to say that unrealized gains and losses are unimportant. On the contrary, unrealized gains and losses determine the overall value of your portfolio and are a large part of what you assess in measuring performance, along with any income generated by your investments. In fact, many discussions of performance in the financial press, especially regarding stocks, focus entirely on these price changes over time.

CHAPTER 10

GET STARTED! A STEP-BY-STEP GUIDE TO SUCCESS

"The secret of getting ahead is getting started."-- *Mark Twain*

Following each woman's story, I mentioned what the suggested solutions were, and in most cases, a Financial Analysis was one of the components of the solution. One of the fundamentals of fixing any situation is an analysis of the problem, to fix or improve our financial life is no different. You must take a baseline analysis to understand where you are and then determine if there are weaknesses and issues to be repaired. In reading this book, one thing may have become evident. Although the book is about investing for women, the truth is, total money management supports investing. Investing is the act of committing money or capital to an endeavor with the expectation of obtaining additional income or profit. If you have investments but you haven't considered all the other issues involved in total money management, you may not be maximizing your usage of money, which is the primary reason to invest. So where do you start on this journey to total empowerment through investing?

Personal Financial Statements

So how do you start? First, take a moment to pray or meditate, or perhaps both, and mentally prepare and commit to putting yourself in a better financial position. Wealth and financial security are as much a mindset as they are strategy and discipline. The first thing you should do after adjusting your mindset is to gather all your financial documents. This should include bank statements for all accounts, your latest retirement and investment account statements, the page called "declaration page" for your homeowner's and auto insurance, your life insurance policies, check stubs, bills, your check register, loan documents, mortgage documents, credit card statements, and anything else related to your money. With this information, you want to prepare what is known as personal financial statements. If you have applied for a loan, the application included a version of this. Please don't fret. This is not hard to do and once you are done, you will be lightyears ahead of most people in managing and investing your money. Tell your friends, "I was working on my personal financial statements over the weekend" and watch how popular you become!

The first financial statement is your balance sheet. A balance sheet documents where you are financially now. If you've taken an accounting class you know a balance sheet shows your assets compared to your liabilities, or said differently, what you own minus what you owe. The difference is your net worth, or put another way, if you were to sell everything you own and pay off all your debts, your net worth is what you have left. Again, start throwing the word net worth around with friends and see your popularity increase!

Please note I have easy to use forms to complete your budget and personal financial statements. Email me at *mark@authormarkaparksjr.com* ***and I will send them to you for free.***

To prepare your statements, gather all your information about your assets. You may ask, exactly what are assets? Assets are what you own. This includes cash, your home, cars, and significant personal property like jewelry and furnishings. To setup the balance sheet, it would be best to use an Excel spreadsheet. If you don't know how to use Excel or you don't have a computer, don't worry, a hand-written document will work, too. Start with your most liquid asset, which is your cash. On the left margin, write cash and next to it write in the total amount of cash you have on hand and in all your cash accounts. This includes checking, savings, money market accounts, and if you have money under the mattress or in a wall safe, include it here also. Next you will add your investment accounts. Start with those outside of your retirement accounts.

On the next line, put your retirement accounts. All the preceding are considered cash accounts. After your cash accounts, the next thing would be your accounts receivable. Most people won't have this, but it is money you are owed, and it should only be the money you expect to collect. The next category is assets that are less liquid. Put the market value of your home. The next line could be the market value of your car, then add anything else like jewelry and furnishings. Don't worry if you still owe money on these assets, it will be offset in another section of your balance sheet with any debts associated with the assets. Total your assets.

Next, you want to tally your liabilities. This does not include bills. This is only for debts having a balance due more than thirty days in the future. The liabilities would include the balances you owe on your mortgage and any second or third mortgages you may have, the balance on your car note, loan balances, including student loans, credit card balances and any other debts you can think of. Now, total your liabilities and subtract the total of your liabilities from your total assets. If the number is positive, congratulations you have a positive net worth! If it is negative, then you have some work to do.

According to Investopedia, the rules of thumb for what your net worth should be is as follows: If you are employed and earning income, the calculation is ((your age) x (annual household income))/ 10, so if you make $100K and you are fifty years old, the calculation would be (50 x 100,000)/10= $500,000. There are many rules of thumb, this is just one to give you an idea of what type of financial shape you're in. Don't worry if you are not on track, you can catch up!

After you completed your balance sheet, you want to do

your income statement, which will lead you to a budget. This will be a separate sheet from your balance sheet. To create an income statement, start with your monthly gross income. It would be best if you used the exact figure from your paystub for this. If you are paid monthly, use the paycheck amount. If you get paid every two weeks, use the paycheck amount multiplied by twenty-six and divided by twelve. The chart below explains how to do this for the varying pay cycles. You will then add any other income you receive, whether it's from a part-time job, a side business, investments, or even child support and alimony. Total all your income.

Next, you are going to document your expenses. Start with housing cost such as mortgage or rent, phone, cable, utilities, lawncare, etc. Then add your expenses like groceries, clothing, childcare, etc. Add charitable giving, transportation costs, leisure cost like vacations and travel, debt, insurance payments, money you put aside, and monthly taxes paid including those withheld from your check. The budget should be so thorough that you are accounting for every dollar. The way to do this is to take your monthly gross income and subtract all the above expenses and uses of money. If at the end you have a lot of money left over, if this feels right, you can stop. However, what I've often seen is people will say, "I don't have that much money left at the end of the month." If this is the case for you, then you need to continue. If you go through this process and you cannot identify where your money goes, then you need to write down or otherwise track your money for a month or so to determine what is happening to your money. Items I have seen missed in the past are entertainment cost, money given to children or other family members and lottery tickets to name a few. Once you can complete this, you will be able to see where all your money is going. As you will see, there are some expenses that are fixed and permanent or long term. You will also see some expenses that are flexible or can be eliminated.

The Budget

At this point, you have an income statement which shows where your money came from and where it went. To turn this document into a budget, you must make some decisions. Ask yourself *Is this how I want to spend my money?* Just because this is what happened doesn't mean it is your preferred scenario. Add another column to the right of the column showing how much you spent on the income statement and put the amount you would prefer to spend on each item monthly on a budgetary basis. This second column will turn into your budget. If your budget shows you have plenty of extra money at the end of the month, you may be in a great place to invest or to pay-off debt.

Are the things you are spending money on really your priorities? Are you spending too much on entertainment? Is your cable bill high and you are never at home to watch TV? Are you spending too much eating out? Do you have vices like gambling or drinking where you are spending more than you should? **Remember, a budget is a plan!** It is for you to direct and control your money. Take my word, if you don't have a plan for your money, someone else will. Why do you think companies spend billions of dollars on advertising? If everyone had a plan for their money, ads would be less effective, except with big data, companies follow your tracks on the internet and if you look for an item you plan to buy, they will make sure it magically appears online when you look at social media or your emails. At least these ads are targeted and may be in line with your priorities.

If your budget shows you spend more money than you have, you are at a deficit. You will need to look at the expenses and make some adjustments to free up money or make more money. One thing I do on a regular basis is contact companies and ask them to lower my interest rate on credit cards or loans, which will lower my payments. Sound crazy or weird? Try it. At least once a year I call credit card companies and ask them to lower my rate. I call the cell phone and cable companies to be given more services for a lower price. Believe it or not, this works at least fifty percent of the time. Typically, the cable company has a plan for a year only or six months, but you could save $30 - $50 per month. The phone companies do the same thing. Credit card companies will often give you a temporary reduction in your interest rate, which lowers your payment. There are people who act like savings of $50 is not worth it and I ask them if they ever found fifty dollars? If they have, they remember it, therefore if you can identify a $50/ month savings for even six months you have saved yourself $300 dollars. Once you have identified these savings, you want to immediately plow them into your debt repayment or your investments. The key to this concept is discipline.

Financial discipline is not easy, but when you master it you will be better off. Beyond popular belief, at some point most of us are going to have to get serious and plan for some long-term outcomes. I understand faith and destiny and all of that, but the Bible clearly says, "Faith without work is dead." Does that apply to finances? Why take the chance, put in some work? When preparing a budget, it's like a diet, you must be realistic. Don't create a budget you know you won't or can't follow. You need to assure you have some room for money you are not going to use constructively, money you're going to blow. It happens, so allow for it in your budget. For instance, for entertainment, treats for yourself, or whatever else you may want to do that doesn't fit into the more stringent categories mentioned earlier. Now you have your personal balance sheet, income statement, and a budget. You are now far ahead of most Americans with your financial planning. You have the tools you need to begin to change your life.

Insurance is Your Financial Foundation

The next thing to consider is making sure you have the

right types and amounts of insurance. Make sure you have insurance on your home, renters or homeowners. Make sure to have insurance on your car. Medical insurance is essential as well. Insurance protects you when catastrophes happen. The reason why I recommend you get insurance before funding an emergency fund and investing is paying insurance is a quick and inexpensive way to get coverage over catastrophes that could happen and require you to spend savings and investments if you don't have insurance. You will soon see why you should be careful about who you listen to about insurance. There are states where auto insurance minimum coverage is $25,000 per person for bodily injury and $50,000 for property damage liability coverage. The insurance companies typically show it as full coverage, $25,000/$50,000. What this means is the *maximum* they will pay are these amounts.

Here is an example of what could happen: You are in Palm Beach, Florida where people drive very expensive cars. You have an accident and you hit a Mercedes Benz that cost $120,000 and you are at fault. The insurance company will pay the $50,000 property damage amount they have agreed to and the insurance company for the person who owns the Mercedes will be coming after you for the additional $70,000. Don't let this happen to you! You can get coverages much higher. I typically recommend the $100,000/$300,000 or more. This amount of insurance, while covering a lot more, doesn't cost much more.

The same concepts apply to homeowner's, renter's, medical, disability and on and on. Having insurance is the best way to secure your finances until you have enough cash to cover any emergencies that may come up. I've always said most emergencies are not emergencies if you have the money. You may take the insurance a little further and make sure you have warrantees on items that make since. I normally don't get warranties on small appliances, but used cars for instance, I always get the warranty. Hopefully, you understand the importance of insurance while building up large savings. One catastrophe could deplete all your savings.

Now let's talk about life insurance. One of the solutions that will come up when talking about investments is insurance. If you recall some of the stories in the book, life insurance came into play or was needed and not available in some of the cases. You remember our twenty-five-year-old wife, Elle, who lost her husband? Helen? Just to name a few. Life insurance is rarely an issue for the octogenarians who die. They're old and unless there is not enough money to bury them, there is no problem. Most of the life insurance challenges come from those who are young and weren't expecting to die when they did.

The other thing about life insurance is it allows you to build an estate quickly. When I refer to an estate, I'm referring to money and assets you leave behind to your heirs. For instance, in the case of the Elle, she needed a large amount of money because her and her child were young. They needed money to sustain them. If a couple tried to save to build an estate, it would take many years to save enough money to sustain the young family when Bert died. Life insurance on the other hand happens immediately. If the Elle would have gotten a life insurance policy, the day it was approved the full-face value would be available at death. So even if she purchased a million-dollar policy and had only paid the first premium of, let's say $100, she would get the one-million-dollar death benefit.

There are at least two schools of thought for life insurance. I am in the school of thought of buy term life insurance and invest the difference. Here is why: Life insurance is to replace income if someone dies. If I had died in my thirties, I would have needed to provide years of income to sustain my family until my sons were out of school and able to support themselves and I needed to provide for my wife. Term life insurance allowed me to get a large policy, like five hundred thousand dollars for under forty dollars per month, and I was into my thirties when I purchased the policy. A cash value policy like a whole life, universal life, or variable life for the same amount of coverage would have cost me hundreds of dollars. As I mentioned, insurance creates an estate immediately, therefore it is most efficient to get the largest amount at the lowest cost. There are a lot of insurance agents who will vehemently disagree with this, partly because the more you spend on insurance, the more they get paid and as you can see cash value policies cost more.

There is a rule used to explain life insurance called the Law of Decreasing Responsibility. What the rule says is when you're young, you have young children who would need a lot of money if you were to die young. The money would be for daily survival in your absence, for a college fund, and to pay off debt. The other part of being young is you typically don't have a lot of money. In this scenario, you need a larger life insurance policy. The rule states as you get older your responsibilities decrease, your mortgage should be less, perhaps your children have finished school and your debts should be low. Also, if you have done things right, you will have significant savings. If you have savings then you don't necessarily need life insurance, at least not large amounts. So, for the coverage of your life I strongly advocate for term life insurance. I would be irresponsible however, if I didn't mention for those who have very large estates, typically more than ten million, there are uses for whole life policies in estate planning. As this book is being written, Congress is trying to repeal estate taxes, so this usage may no longer be an issue at some point.

Another issue is when to buy insurance. Many advisors will tell you if you are single with no children, you shouldn't bother. If you read the preceding women's stories, you will have noticed life can change very quickly and if you really need life insurance, if you are very sick for instance, there is no way you will get it. Life insurance is given to those who have minimal chances of dying before the company makes their money, so if you are seriously ill, you probably won't get it. Therefore, I tend to recommend even if you are single with no kids, you should get at least a small policy, and since I believe in term, the cost should be minimal.

If you are not sure how much life insurance to get, you can use the DIME method. DIME stands for Debt, Income, Mortgage, and Education. As I have mentioned earlier, life insurance is to replace the income of the person who dies, so the first item, debt would suggest that you should have enough life insurance coverage to pay-off the family's debt. Relieving your survivors of debt is a great help to survivors if there is significant debt outstanding.

The next item is income. A portion of the life insurance proceeds should be to cover the deceased's income. A method of doing this would to set up an annuity with a long-term payout to cover the income. This would be an immediate annuity. Mortgage is debt, so the same debt process should be used. Education cost can be determined utilizing tools on the internet. What is not covered in the DIME calculation is burial, so add this. If you have enough life insurance to cover these items, you can be comfortable you left your family in good shape.

Debt Elimination

You may now be asking yourself, "I thought this book was about investing. Why are we talking about debt again?" Well, the process I am taking you through is the best way to prepare to maximize your money. It is a very strategic approach and once you start to implement, you will start to see the benefits manifests themselves repeatedly. The reason why I put debt before savings is simple. If you have a credit card at the time, I am writing this book, the interest rates the bank charges is typically at least 10%. Also, at the time I am writing this book, the interest rate on a Passbook Savings account has an average rate of .12% and a one-year Certificate of Deposit is at 2.60%. Does it make sense to save money at .12% or even 2.60% when you're paying in excess of 10% for a credit card. No, it doesn't make sense.

The best process for eliminating debt is to review all your debts and list starting with the highest interest rate. Many people will pay a little extra on each of their credit cards. A better process is to determine which credit card has the highest interest and put all your extra payment money towards that specific debt until it is paid off. The next step is to be very disciplined. Instead of taking the money you paid for the debt now paid off and buying more clothes or going out to dinner more often you add this money to the payment for the next highest interest debt until it is paid off and repeat this process until all the debt are paid off. Basically, you pay the same amount you paid towards your total debts until they are all paid off. This is called Debt Stacking. I will use a little caution because sometimes debt is so high, you can't wait to pay it all off before an emergency fund is started. In those situations, allocate a portion of money to paying off debt and another portion funding your emergency fund.

The key to this process is to start building discipline around your finances. Many of us have strong work ethics. We believe in giving our all for our jobs and our careers so that we can maximize our earnings potential. Therefore, it only makes sense that we should be equally as focused and concerned about the money we make. Learning to maximize your money once you have received it is a natural progression. Once you are in tune with your money, it helps you make better decisions. If you know your net worth, for instance, then you know what you need to do to increase to get where you need it to be.

Adding Income

Another strategy is to raise your income. There are several ways to do this. One option is to get a side hustle, also known as a part-time business. The other option is to work a part time job. Another option is to invest money to bring in more income, which could manifest itself in many ways. I have always had a side business due to job insecurity that was instilled in me at a young age. When I was in my twenties, I had a boss who didn't care for me and some of my co-workers because we had college degrees and she didn't. She always gave us a hard time and at the time, I had an apartment and a car loan. I also didn't have anywhere to go if I lost my job and couldn't afford to pay rent. At that point, decided I didn't want to be beholden and reliant on someone else for my livelihood. Due to my job situation, I started a small videotaping business where my partner and I would make about $1,500 per month. I also took on a part-time job. I had no desire to have my life determined by others. To this day, I have always continued to have alternate sources of income.

Choosing a Financial Advisor

Most of what I have discussed up to this point can be handled by yourself with the guidance of this book. I do, however, advise you to reach out to me or if you have a financial advisor, you reach out to them when you embark on savings and investments, especially the investment side. If you plan on investing to make additional money, make sure to do your due diligence. This takes me to my next solution, a financial advisor. Financial advisors come from many different disciplines and they may have different experience. For instance, most of my career I have been a Certified Public Accountant (CPA). As a CPA, I have consulted people on business operations, tax planning, succession planning and other business-related consulting. I subsequently became licensed in life insurance and obtained multiple security licenses. The additional licenses and training gave me a basis to consult people in investing and, quite honestly, most financial areas.

I must take a moment here to advise you that you want to be clear about your advisor's experiences and qualifications. There are CPAs who don't know anything about taxes other than what they learned in school and what they needed to know to pass the test. I know many

CPAs who don't know about and don't like to do taxes. There are also CPAs who don't know about investments. Also, as I mentioned earlier in the book, there are times when people put themselves out as financial advisors, but they are really just insurance salesmen. If they don't have the proper license, they can't talk to you about investments; therefore, it should be no surprise when an insurance product is their answer to your investment need.

The other thing is being aware of the advisor who is beholden, or the technical term is captive. Captive agents are those who are employed by a company and can only sell products of their company. If an agent/advisor can only sell the products of their company, every solution may not be the best for you because all their products might not be the best products for all investment concerns. Having a captive advisor is not bad, but this will require you to ask questions to assure they have your best interest in mind, not just theirs. There are also advisors who are fee based who are not affiliated with any company. Fee-based advisors charge a fee and tell you what to invest in, but they don't sell products. The other none fee-based advisors make their money off the commissions of the products they sell, but they can sell products from many companies. It is important you know how your advisor gets paid. As I have reiterated in this book, advisors often have their own financial well-being in mind, so knowing how they are making their money will give you an idea of their motivation for certain suggestions. Needless to say, choosing an advisor is a challenging but important process.

So, what questions should you ask a potential advisor?

As I've mentioned, many women have stated they don't know what questions to ask an advisor. Financial advisors are no different than most other advisors you may utilize. You have a problem, or a concern and you need a solution. Both in taxes and in investing, I have always felt like I was the doctor that could heal your challenges. You have a need. It may be to save money for college for your children. It may be to save for your retirement. You may want to make sure your family is covered in the event there is a crisis, whether its death, sickness, an auto accident, a housefire, disability, or anything else that could happen. On the lighter side, you may want to save for a dream house or a dream vacation. Perhaps you want to be out of debt or you may just want to bring in some investment income, so you don't have to work. Or perhaps as in many cases, it is all the above. Just like when you go to the doctor, you tell the advisor where you are and where you want to go and what challenges exist. Any good advisor will do an assessment based on real data and then they will make recommendations. You want to be honest when the advisor is trying to help you, so the solutions recommended fit well. You also want to verify fundamental information about the advisor, like her education, licenses, certifications and years in business. You also want to understand the organization she works for, their financial strength, assets under management, and years in business. **Always, always ask for references!**

I have spent significant time and energy researching and exploring the issue of women and investing. Educating and helping women through this process has had a positive effect on me. I believe focusing on women can also positively affect our whole communities!

So, what has been discussed is to identify your goals and challenges and let the advisor prepare the analysis. The analysis will most likely result in a plan you may not be able to totally implement but a good plan will be a road map to get you where you need to be. Even once you have a completed plan, your input is still required. The plan should tell you what your goals are and what you need to do to achieve them. Many plans, depending on your goals, will have items requiring a lot more money, possibly more than you have.

You will want your advisor to do a thorough review of the plan with you, not just a sell of all the products identified. If you are dealing with a fee-based advisor, he will not sell products. They will tell you what you need to move forward with and possibly the brokers with whom you should work with. You certainly want to ask why the professional they have referred you to makes the most sense for you. Now, even though I have talked about the steps to choose an advisor, I will proceed with steps you should take whether the advisor guides you through or you continue to be guided by this book.

Goals

Now that you have a baseline where your finances are, it is time to set goals. This should be the fun part! Yes, you should have goals to eliminate debt. You should also have goals for accumulating savings in my opinion, and if you have children, you may want to have goals to assure they have what they need, college being a typical goal for savings, but you should also have fun here. What do you really want? Where do you want to live? Do you want to travel? Buy a home? A car? Do you want to live on an island? Do you want to have a million dollars or more? I can tell you **all your goals can come true**. I am a true believer people get what they desire if they plan and work towards it. I've always told my children it is not a matter of if you get what you desire, it's when. You may not become a millionaire over night, but with proper planning and execution, it can happen.

When you set your goals, they should be SMART goals. SMART stands for Specific, Measurable, Attainable, Realistic, and Timely. SMART goals are complete. By being specific, they are identifying something specific. For instance, instead of saying you want to travel, you should state you want to travel to Honolulu, Hawaii. In being measurable, you want to say when and how long. For instance, I want to go to Honolulu, Hawaii in June 2020 for a week. Having a timeframe and a duration is measurable and offers a clear picture into what your goal is.

Attainable is very important as well. I once had a couple who made a total of $30,000 annually, and one of their goals was to purchase a Leer jet. The price of a Leer jet starts at about $20 million. I know I have said you can attain anything, but it would be prudent to start with goals which have some semblance of being attained in ten years or less. They were a very spiritual couple and believed in miracles, as do I, but your financial plan should not be based solely on Divine Intervention. If it happens, that's great. To get you motivated, start with goals that can be attained quickly so you can gain some momentum. The Leer jet example speaks to the realistic criteria also. Again, your goals are your goals, but making them realistic helps you attain them and will help you build momentum and confidence. For a goal to be timely, there must be a timeline set when it should be attained. For the Honolulu trip, the timing might be to have the money available six months in advance of the travel date, so you have ample hotels and flights to choose from.

So, have some fun! Plan a great vacation. Plan to buy that car you always wanted. Buy a piece of jewelry you always wanted, accumulate the down payment for the home you want, or buy or start a business, but remember, be SMART! Don't build up hard to pay back debt and for the smaller items pay for them in cash. Once you have all your goals, depending upon how many you have, you may want to prioritize and leave some off for the future. If you only have a few, you should arrange them in the order of when they should be achieved, with the goals with the closest achievement dates being first.

Next, you put the estimated cost for each and determine how much you need to save each month to achieve the goals by the desired dates. Once you have determined the monthly amount needed, if it is within your reach, get started. Caution, I did say have fun, but remember good money management suggests you should have an emergency fund, eliminate debt, and you will have a plan for retirement, then and *only* then, should you go for the more fun goals!

Savings

I have talked to you about terms and concepts to make you look brilliant and impressive to your friends, here is another! At some point, you will want to open a brokerage account. Many people associate a brokerage account with the super-rich because some brokerages require you to have large deposits to open an account. Most brokerages require at least one to five thousand to open an account; however, there are discount brokerages like TD Ameritrade where there is typically no minimum beginning deposit. A brokerage account will allow you to easily purchase stocks, bonds, and mutual funds quickly.

To open an account, just go online and sign up. If you are starting the account with a balance of less than one thousand dollars, I recommend that you set up the account to make regular deposit at least monthly. Once the account is set-up and you have a balance of at least five-hundred dollars, you can begin to invest.

Choosing a Stock

You may ask yourself *Where do I start?* First, we have talked about stocks and the many different options in chapter eight, "Types of Investments.". You can determine what you want to invest in based on information in that chapter or you may already have a company in mind you want to invest in. If you don't have a company in mind, think about products or services you buy for yourself or your children. Think about what people buy a lot of. Think about companies you know are successful.

To give you an example of how this works, some years ago I wanted to invest, and I thought about what was popular. It was a time when smart phones seemed to be gaining popularity. So, I Googled "Apple" to see how much the stock in the iPhone manufacturer cost. At the time, one share of Apple stock cost around $200 per share. With a small amount of money to invest, I would not have gotten a lot of traction with a stock this expensive. How about Microsoft? Microsoft was a little less at $120 per share, but still without a lot to invest I wouldn't be able to purchase a significant number of shares.

Then I looked back at my smartphone because I could tell people were really buying a lot of smart phones. I thought about the components of smart phones like, the batteries, the screens, and the microprocessors. I looked up these components and decided to go with the microprocessors. I did a little more research and found out who made the microprocessors used in cell phones and researched those stocks. There is a lot of information available about stocks online. I chose a microprocessor company that was doing well, and the price was only $17 per share.

At the date of writing this chapter, the stock was selling at $43 per share. As you can see this was more than double. It is about a 250% gain. To quantify this, if I invested $1,700 for one hundred shares, my investment is now worth $4,300 two years later. I am not suggesting you should invest in microprocessors, nor am I suggesting you will have a similar experience with this or any other investment, I just wanted to illustrate the process.

You may want to know about my analysis. I read about the stocks on the brokerages website and most brokers will have a tool on their site with several views of analysts stating whether the stock is something you should buy, sell, or avoid. You can also go online and find a tremendous amount of information about companies. Remember some people equate the stock market with gambling in Las Vegas. The reality is if you invest in strong companies that make money, your investment should be fine. If you don't want to go through this, the brokerages all have brokers who can choose and recommend stocks for you. If you choose to go with a broker, make sure she understands what your goals are.

Once you choose a company, now you need to determine how many shares you want to purchase. Some stocks require minimum purchases, but I haven't experienced this lately. If you have more money once you have decided how much of the first stock to buy, you can go through the process again and choose another stock or several more depending upon how much money you have and your objectives.

Bonds

I've talked about diversification, which means you should invest in different types of stocks as well as bonds. Bond analysis is different, yet basically you want to choose those that are paying the highest interest when you are dealing with investment grade bonds. Other bonds may pay higher interest, but if they are not investment grade, it is more likely they may not be able to pay back your principal. Therefore, you may want professional guidance when purchasing bonds. Federal government bonds are the safest investments because they are guaranteed by the full-faith and credit of the United States Government.

In addition to government bonds, there are corporate bonds also. Companies can get capital by selling stock or by issuing bonds. As I mentioned earlier, bonds are debt and stocks are ownership in a company. When you purchase bonds, you must be sure the company is strong enough to pay you back. You can use the bonds credit rating and if it is investment grade meaning it is rated "BBB" or better, your chances are better you can be repaid.

There are other considerations when you are investing. Will you buy the securities for a long-term, short-term, or take a hybrid approach? For most people who are saving for long-term goals, it is recommended you hold securities for a long-term of a year or more. You may want to set limits. For instance, with the microprocessor stock I purchased above, I could have set a limit so once the stock doubled for instance I would sell. Understand when you sell a stock and make money, you are taxed on your gains.

Also, understand there are instances when stocks decrease in value, so you could set a lower limit too. Using the microprocessor example, you could decide you will sell once the stock goes down to $15 dollars per share allowing you to minimize your losses. In both examples, you can have the brokerage set-up the limits and the transactions will happen automatically when the limits are met.

When you invest in stocks and bonds, you want to make sure it is money you can afford to lose. If you choose well, you most likely won't lose all your money, but if it is money you need for living expenses, it will make it harder for you to follow the primary rule of investing well. The rule is: **"Buy low, sell high."**

The example with the microprocessor is a perfect example of this. I bought the stock at $17 per share and could have sold it at $43 per share and made $2,600. On the flip side, what if I bought the stock at $43 per share and the stock dropped to $17 per share an I sold it. In this instance, I would have done the opposite of what you are supposed to do. I bought high and sold low. Of course, if you determine a stock may not recover, you will want to sell it before you lose all of your money, but this is a harder process if you struggle to suffer temporary loses because you really need the money, Stocks fluctuate in price and the best investors don't look at every stock every day and worry about temporary losses. Please understand other than dividends paid, you don't realize a gain or lose money with stock until you sell it.

Now that you have your plan of action, understand stocks, bonds and mutual funds, and you have your foundational insurance policies in place, it is time for savings! Savings are a fundamental part of financial security and a mindset. There are people who don't have the discipline to watch money accumulate and every time they have a small balance, they spend it. I had a client who set up a mutual fund for savings over twenty years ago. She deposits one hundred dollars per month. She currently has less than fifty dollars in this account and upon review, every month she takes the money back out. This is not a good idea because there are fees associated with investing in mutual funds. I have recommended she change her strategy, but she only adjusts temporarily. When I counsel people on savings, I always recommend they start with an affordable fixed amount on a monthly or bi-weekly basis. When they get a raise in salary, I suggest they add at least a portion of the raise to their savings immediately. If you were already living off a smaller amount of money, it wouldn't cause any additional distress. There were years when I added my entire raise to my retirement savings.

Emergency Fund

So where do you start with savings? You start by building an emergency fund. There are several schools of thought on what your emergency fund should be. I typically recommend you have enough money to cover six months of expenses. When I was younger, it made sense to keep all this money in a money market fund, but as I got older, my perspective changed. When I was younger, my monthly expenses were less than $2,000 per month. Keeping $12,000 in a low-yielding money market account made more sense. As I got older and had expenses of approximately $5,000 per month, keeping all the emergency funding in low-yielding accounts made less sense. I would recommend three months of money in checking and low-yielding accounts and placing the rest in conservative income mutual funds yielding more returns but allowing you to access the money relatively quickly when needed.

The worst emergency to deal with is unemployment. The majority of other emergencies will not require such large amounts. Typical household emergencies do not exceed an immediate need of more than ten thousand dollars. If the emergencies are much larger, they may require a credit solution, like a loan. Once you have your emergency fund you feel will more secure. You can be more flexible if for instance you take a new job that stretches your abilities and it doesn't work out, you have money to fall back on and as was discussed earlier, you may not have to connect with a mate you don't particularly care for in order to sustain your lifestyle. I assure you, having some financial stability will give you a new level of confidence and security.

Retirement

Now you have an emergency fund, you want to start to focus on your retirement accounts. Now I will say, you definitely need an emergency fund and it is a preference, but if you work at a job where they are matching your retirement contributions, you will want to start saving for retirement as soon as possible. In some situations, it may be recommended you apportion part of your savings to your emergency fund and a portion to retirement. Keep in mind there is no a one size fits all approach to investing and a good advisor will help you through this. For retirement savings, I would suggest, at minimum, you contribute up to the amount your job matches. If you have additional money, you will want to max out your contributions to your retirement accounts. The reason to maximize your savings in your employer's plan is because the fees are typically lower, and the accounts have tax advantages. You will want to verify this is the case, it is with most larger employers.

If you work for a government or a school, their plans may

have a fixed amount they withdraw from your pay each month. The standard amount when I worked for a government in Ohio was 10% and the employer added 10.5%. The 10% deduction may not be enough based on your required lifestyle in retirement, so governments typically offer secondary plans where you can have an additional tax advantaged deduction. For schools it's typically a 403B plan and for governmental entities, it's a 457 plan. The great thing about these plans is they are pre-tax. So, what does that mean? Pre-tax savings come out of your check before taxes are calculated, so if you make $2,000 per month and you had 10% coming out of your check, they would take out $200 per month.

Without going into complex calculations and explanations of tax withholdings, I will tell you even though $200 was taken from your pay, when you get your take home pay the difference will be less than $200. The other bonus to this setup is when you file your income taxes at the end of the year, you are not taxed on the money that went into your retirement account. **Now remember, there is no free lunch.** At retirement, when you receive your savings you will be taxed on the money not previously taxed. The rationale for this is in retirement, your income will be lower; therefore, being taxed on the money at this time would have less of an impact. The reality is I haven't seen this happen often because when people are younger, they have deductions like children and mortgage interest. If they have managed their lives in a traditional way, at retirement they don't have either of these things;

therefore, they are subjected to significant taxation. Needless to say, money management for retirees could be another book, so we will leave it here.

College Planning

For college savings, there will be a few options. My favorite is a 529 plan. The great thing about 529 plans is you can contribute large amounts and you maintain control of your money, unlike the other popular college savings plans, Uniform Gift to Minors and Uniform Transfer to Minors Act, better known as UGMAs and UTMAs. The problem with these plans is when the child reaches the age of majority, the money belongs to the child; therefore, even though you saved the money for their college expenses, if they decided they wanted to buy a corvette instead, they could. Many state plans are set-up as UGMAs and they allow state tax benefits; therefore, you will want to evaluate the benefits of each plan before deciding.

Picking a Mate

We talked about how to pick an advisor, but one of the mistakes many women make is in choosing their mates. Are you thinking, *I can't believe he went there*? Well I did, and I will at least talk about this briefly. I have sat down with a lot of women and when we go through their budget, there is sometimes a gap. Budgeting, which is an essential part of money managements, is something I go through with clients very thoroughly. There have been times where there is a large amount of unexplained expenses that can't be identified and then, he walks in: The No-Account man that is more of a liability than anything else. We love who we love, but if you take the time to strategically choose your mate, you want to choose one who is financially strong or at minimum, not a liability. Had I written this book twenty years ago, I would have said it is okay for a man to choose a woman who has no financial attributes, but now, I also believe men should be cognizant of what the financial situation is of their mates. I am not suggesting choosing a mate without money management abilities is not acceptable, but I am suggesting it should at least be a part of data gathering when a mate is chosen to continue forward with. A very large percentage of marriages and relationships end because of money; therefore, the conversations should be had **right in the beginning!** Please understand divorce is probably one of the challenges that ruins many peoples' financial status. Often in divorce, one party files bankruptcy and the other party must follow suit. Otherwise, they would be stuck with all the bills.

Since I took time out to talk about mates, I would be remiss if I didn't talk about family members as well. Many of those who are not good money managers or don't invest are that way due to the training they received from their families. Therefore, if you are in a situation where your family is not supportive of where you are going, you may want to look at why that may be. If you come from a family that hasn't done well financially living the proverbial "paycheck to paycheck" lifestyle, you may want to limit the amount of advice you take from them. I can't tell you how many people I have seen in bad situations because of advice they received from family members without financial acumen.

Wills and Trusts

In this book, I have restricted it primarily to money management and investing. It should be clear however, there are other issues that should be taken care of to have your financial house in order. The issue of wills and trusts is one of those issues. Most people know what a will is, but trust is not as common. A trust is an arrangement whereby a person (a trustee) holds property as its nominal owner for one or more beneficiaries. One of the most publicized cases of the usage of a trust is when hotel heiress, Leona Helmsley died and left her 8-year old Maltese Trouble $12 million in a trust. Clearly the dog could not manage the money, so the trustee distributed the money to Helmsley's brother, who was given custody of the dog, when the dog needed something. Wills and trusts are an essential part of planning but the text to explain this would easily fill the pages of a whole new book! What I will say about wills and trusts is: **You should have them!**

When I consulted with my very wealthy clients where estate taxes were an issue, I would talk to them about an Estate Plan, which included many levels of the trust, and the will was the catch-all to make sure anything *not* covered in the trust was covered by the will. For basic clients, a will makes sense to assure your assets go where you want upon your death. Another type of will for average investors is a living will to assure if you have medical issues near the end of life, your wishes will be handled correctly.

As I mentioned above, having a will can make sure your assets go where you like. I can speak to this personally as a child who lost out twice on the wealth of my parents due to probate rules. If you get remarried, for the sake of your children, do some estate planning for when you die! Here is why: If you have children prior to being married, whether it's from a previous marriage or you had children before you were married, beware! The way the law works in most states is the spouse trumps the children. For example, your mother and father were married for many years and your father dies. Over the years they were married they accumulated a lot of wealth. Well when your father dies, let's assume you're a minor, everything will typically go to your mom, which is normally fine because she should have your best interest in mind. Next, your mother, who is still attractive and desirable, is courted and she finds another mate. Regardless if this mate is wealthy or not, your rightful inheritance is at risk! For this example, let's assume the new mate doesn't have his own money. If your mother dies after they have wed, all the wealth built up by your mother and father goes to the new husband. Not the best situation, right?

But here's an even *worse* scenario from my perspective: Let's assume your mom and her new husband are in an auto accident. Your mom dies immediately, and your stepfather dies a few months later. Because of the way the law works, at least in Ohio, due to your mom dying first, the money would technically go to her husband, even if he had never regained consciousness. When he dies, the money goes to his children, **not you**. If this doesn't concern you, then don't worry about a will. If it does at least concern you a little, you want to have a will created for you to ensure your money goes where you want. In this situation, had your father had a will and estate plan, all of this could have been avoided. He could have put money in a trust for you and at some point, it would come to you. Again, this is a complex discussion, but it needs to be addressed in your financial planning.

CHAPTER 11

CUSTOMIZED ANSWERS

"If the challenge exists, so must the solution."--
Rona Mlnarik

Single Ladies

I've discussed how to get started. Now, I want to provide you with some additional insight into how your marital status could require a more customized approach. I was asked why I used this approach and the reason is taxes, investments, and retirement accounts all have rules based on whether or not you are married. Because of your marital status, there are different approaches to be taken. There is no one-size-fits-all solution for any classification of women, but their characteristics, such as being single or married, present different issues and solutions.

When I talk about single women, I need to define it. I will use the definition of a "single woman" as one who supports herself, has no children, and primarily takes care of her own affairs. This could be a great place to be and many single women relish this existence. The good thing about being this version of single is the freedom and the limited responsibility to others.

A single woman in this category who makes a good amount of money can have everything she may want including investments, a nice home, a nice car, and a great wardrobe. Because they are only responsible for themselves, women in this category sometimes don't see the urgency or need for financial planning and investing. When you can buy and do what you want, saving money may not be a concern. Hopefully from this book you have been able to understand life changes do in fact happen, and that being prepared to pivot when it does is important.

Let's think back to some of the stories. Consider Jean: she didn't think she would have any children but ended up with a child and the need to provide for them while she was alive and, in the event,, something happened to her, and it did, she needed to be prepared financially. Remember the many women I discussed who lost their jobs or had financial reversals due to business failures? What about one who becomes ill or at some point wants to retire? Will they have enough money when the income stops? My goal is not to scare you but to provide you insight into why you may want to prepare as a single person. If you are like me, once you attain a certain lifestyle, there is no desire to go down a rung or two; therefore, a little planning could go a long way.

So as a single woman, what should you do? The first thing you should do is develop a plan. **You could use this book and develop a plan on your own, you can hire an advisor, or you can use online tools. There is a list of resources in the back of the book.** Next, you want to prepare for emergencies. Make sure if you own a home you have homeowner's insurance and if you rent, you have renter's insurance. Make sure to have insurance on your car. Medical insurance is essential as well. Insurance protects you when catastrophes happen; it is the foundation of your financial well-being. Then, you want to build an emergency fund. It is recommended you have six months of liquid, easily accessible money to cover emergencies or job or business losses. When money is available to cover emergencies, they become more of an occurrence rather than an emergency.

Caution: If you have a lot of debt, you will want to put a large portion of your money toward said debt and some towards the emergency fund. Having debt for extended amounts of time is problematic for many reasons. Once you have taken care of the emergency fund, you want to put retirement savings in place. If you have a job offering a retirement plan, you should start there. You should participate in the plan, at minimum, to the level where they match your contributions. If you do all of this, as a single lady, you have put yourself in a position to be able to be in great shape for the long term.

All the above is essential and like in many situations when something is required, it is not exciting. However, once you have taken care of your emergency fund and retirement, it's time to move to more exciting things like your goals and dreams. Identify what you want in the future. It could be vacations, a new car or home, or a luxury item you've always wanted. Figure out how much it will cost, when you want it, and then develop a plan to save the money to buy the item or at least make a significant down payment. It's very exciting to see your dreams and financial goals come into fruition.

I have talked a lot about what savings you should have, but little about investing. Once you have gone beyond the emergency fund, which should be invested in a liquid and safe bank product, the rest should be invested in one of the many investments detailed in chapter 8.

As you move forward you can decide to increase insurance coverages and savings. The best way to do this is to envision where you would like to see yourself in the future and set your goals based on that.

Single Moms

Now for the single moms with the additional responsibility of children, it is no longer an option to purchase life insurance. If something happens to you, who will take care of your children? Will they have enough to take care of them without any additional cash? Insurance will be able to address this and if the caregiver does have enough to provide for your child as you would have, the money can go to the child when they are in college or an adult.

The great thing about being a mom is most moms have strong maternal instincts and put their children first naturally; therefore, to convince a woman with children she should put something in place to take care of them should be a no-brainer. I understand life insurance sometimes seems like a waste of money, but when you don't have it and really need it, the importance is evident. To make purchasing life insurance easier, buy term life insurance. Term life insurance is relatively inexpensive, and it does exactly what life insurance is supposed to do, to provide money when you die. If you have young children, you want to get at least a 20-year term, so you can be covered until your children are grown. With children you also want to make sure you have medical insurance and you want to have all the savings accounts we mentioned above for single women without children.

In some cases, single women with children have a tighter money situation than our free-spirited women with no children; therefore, careful planning is required because mistakes could result in tough times for the women and her children. My hope is the man who helped create the children helps with the expenses. There may be the random man who will complain about child support and sometime suggest the woman is spending his money on herself and not the children, yet I always push back and say,

"If she has the children all the time, the man's money isn't enough to squabble over. She is definitely spending money on your children, unless they are being neglected."

I have been in many arguments with men about this issue. As a man who raised my children in our home their whole lives, I have little patience for a man who complains about the money being taken from them through the court system. I have two boys who played sports and in any given year they needed basketball shoes, cleats, and miscellaneous equipment, this would sometimes eclipse the amount of money some men are spending for the entire year through the child support system. But again, I digress. If the man is helping, it's great.

Married

Now for you married women, the needs are the same, but of course, everything should be expanded. In the married scenario life insurance is not an option, children or not. Most couples live off the total of both salaries, therefore if one of the two were to die, the other would need to replace the income of their spouse. The age-old argument about the worth of a stay-at-home spouse needs to be valued here, also. Consider this: even if the woman or man is a stay-at-home parent, there is a cost to be replaced if they were to die. If the sole provider is like I was when my children were younger, he would spend a lot of time working while my wife took care of the home and the children. Consider this: if my wife would have died, I would have needed a daycare, transportation, and someone to feed and teach the children, not to mention all the other things she did that were essential. These are not services you can get for free, so even if a spouse is a stay at home parent, there needs to be money to replace what they were doing.

The other challenge with marriage is assuring the spouse is on the same page. If you have a mate that is not willing to be forward thinking as it relates to money, this can be a big challenge in the relationship. We have all seen where relationships fall apart due to finances.

Divorcees

Divorce is a challenge I have never had to deal with personally but have seen many times in the lives of my clients. One of the biggest challenges I have seen in divorce is when one of the former spouse's files for bankruptcy. This happens often. If you understand the financial arrangement of a marriage, you will understand it's like a business partnership. **Just like in a business partnership, if the couple has debts that were part of the marriage, and if one of the spouses does not pay, then the other spouse is one hundred percent liable.** For this reason, when a former spouse files bankruptcy, the remaining former spouse must also, or they will be liable to pay all the debts accumulated during the marriage and discharged in bankruptcy by the other spouse. Please consult a legal professional before making a decision on filing bankruptcy.

Other than the issue with the bankruptcy, the divorcee would use an approach like the single woman or the single moms.

Widowers

Now this area requires certain financial moves, but the use of a lawyer is certainly advised when talking about widows. I'll start with a basic scenario where the widow had one husband who had one wife. In this situation, other than the grief accompanied with it, the process is somewhat simple. The assets left by the husband transfer to the wife with little difficulty in most states and from an estate tax perspective, there are no taxes due. The challenge comes in with re-titling the assets. The wife will need to send death certificates and other documentation to the companies holding the investments to have the husband removed from the accounts and have her name added.

The other challenge is now this widow who may not have been involved in the investing is now in charge. At this point I advise the widow to identify a third party to work with her in talking to the current advisor if they didn't have a prior relationship. The reason for this is sometimes investment advisors can be like used car salesmen; if they think they have an inexperienced person they're working with, they might try to take advantage of the widow. Before this happens, I have recommended in this book a wife who is not involved in the investments and taxes at least on an annual basis have a conversation with the husband, preferably with the advisor in attendance, to discuss where the couple is as it relates to investments and taxes. This process will at minimum acquaint the wife with the advisors and some level of understanding about what is going on before it is too late.

The widow's situation can be more complex when children and multiple marriages are involved, especially if one or two of the spouses have children outside of the marriage. **The best advice I can give is to be conscious of your situation.** There are a few basic things you can do if you are in a second marriage, whether it's yours or your spouses. You will want to make sure all the beneficiary information is appropriate. There is probably no worse situation than when a man dies and because he never changed his beneficiary, the ex-wife gets all his assets and the current wife gets nothing. Sound like a bad situation? You bet it is! Some states have put in provisions to help avoid this, but your best bet is to get the paperwork in order.

The other challenge is when there are children outside of the marriage. This scenario can get very difficult and complex and peoples' feelings can amplify at the time of tragedy, therefore the best advice I can give is if you enter a relationship with any of these challenges, you have a discussion early in the relationship with a lawyer who is knowledgeable in these areas.

The Journey is Never Ending

"I Don't Need Prince Charming to Have My Happy Ending."--Katy Perry

Congratulations on reading and completing this initial quest to financial freedom. Having gone through "The Gift." You have been empowered to improve your financial situation whether you're young, old, married, single or divorced. You have learned about the pillars of a strong financial house and you have learned terms and types of investments. You have seen the stories and the consequences of some tragic financial situations and some very good situations.

Now let me reveal the five major obstacles that stop women from achieving financial success:

1. The lack of a concise financial plan
2. Keeping up with bills and managing debt
3. How and when to select a financial advisor
4. Understanding investments as a means of enhancing financial success
5. Personal relationships that harm financial sustainability

These are the most prevalent obstacles women have said they have based on hundreds of interviews and surveys and I am happy to say, they have all been addressed in the text of this book.

Tell me, what would it look like if you achieved your ultimate financial goal? How would you live? Where would you live? Would you have a job? Would you have the job you have now? What would you do for your family? What projects and causes would you support?

Is this too many questions to consider? If it is, understand when you have financial freedom you have a lot of options. Remember Oprah's quote at the beginning of the book? It said,

"What material success does is provide you with the ability to concentrate on other things that really matter. And being able to make a difference not only in your own life, but in other people's lives."

I'm asking you to use this book as a continued source of reference, share it, re-read it, buy more and gift them to your family, friends, and associates. Keep in mind the road to financial freedom is a journey not a destination. Please help to put the women in your life in a position to win financially so we can continue to change the world for the better. Thanks for your support!

Sincerely,

Mark

Guide to Resources

In this section I have included governmental and quasi-governmental sites and organizations with a lot of information about money management and investing. There is a lot of information to help you avoid scams and bad products in addition to how to look up people who market and sell investments, so you can avoid negative experiences. This section also has resources to help you manage your finances and save money.

Investor.gov

https://www.investor.gov/ Brought to you by the Security and Exchange Commission's (SEC) Office of Investor Education and Advocacy, Investor.gov is your online resource to help you make sound investment decisions and avoid fraud.

The SEC's Office of Investor Education and Advocacy (OIEA) is dedicated to serving the needs of individual investors. It has three functional units:

1. The Office of Investor Education carries out the SEC's investor education program, which include producing and distributing educational materials, leading educational seminars and investor-oriented events, and partnering with federal agencies, state regulators, consumer groups and self-regulatory organizations on investor literacy initiatives.

2. <u>The Office of Investor Assistance</u> responds to questions, complaints, and suggestions from the members of the public. The Office handles investment-related complaints and questions from tens of thousands of individual investors and others every year. Investors may contact them through their online <u>complaint forms</u> or <u>question form</u>, or their hotline, (800) SEC-0330 (toll-free in the U.S.) to ask questions on a wide range of securities-related topics, to complain about problems with your investments or your financial professionals, or to suggest improvements to the agency's regulations and procedures.

3. The <u>Office of the Chief Counsel</u> creates educational materials on securities-related topics for the public (including for Investor.gov, the SEC's website designed for individual investors) and provides advice to OIEA on securities and administrative law issues.

If investors have complaints regarding a broker or investment adviser, they will contact the company or individual to find out what happened. Sometimes, this results in a satisfactory resolution of the complaint. Other times, it's unclear who is right and who is wrong. In that case, they let investors know their legal options and how they can pursue a resolution on their own.

Their specialists also research and provide information on a range of topics, such as whether a broker or investment professional is properly licensed to do business, or whether a company is registered with the SEC.

They cannot tell investors what investments to make but they can provide unbiased information on investment decisions and how to protect yourselves from securities fraud or abuse.

Securities and Exchange Commission (SEC)

https://www.sec.gov - The mission of the SEC is to protect investors, maintain fair, orderly, and efficient markets and facilitate capital formation. The SEC strives to promote a market environment that is worthy of the public's trust.

Securities Investor Protection Corporation (SIPC)

https://www.sipc.org - Brokerage firm failures are rare. If it happens, SIPC protects the securities and cash in your brokerage account up to $500,000. The $500,000 protection includes up to $250,000 protection for cash in your account to buy securities.

Financial Industry Regulatory Agency (FINRA)

http://www.finra.org/ - FINRA is dedicated to investor protection and market integrity through effective and efficient regulation of broker-dealers.

FINRA is not part of the government. They are a not-for-profit organization authorized by Congress to protect America's investors by making sure the broker-dealer industry operates fairly and honestly.

They do this by:

- writing and enforcing rules governing the activities of all registered broker-dealer firms and registered brokers in the U.S.;
- examining firms for compliance with those rules;
- fostering market transparency; and
- educating investors.

Their regulation plays a critical role in America's financial system—by enforcing high ethical standards, bringing the necessary resources and expertise to regulation and enhancing investor safeguards and market integrity—all at no cost to taxpayers.

Every investor in America relies on one thing: fair financial markets. That's why FINRA works every day to ensure that:

- every investor receives the **basic protections** they deserve;
- anyone who sells a securities product has been **tested, qualified and licensed**;
- every securities product advertisement used is **truthful**, and not misleading;
- any securities product sold to an investor is **suitable** for that investor's needs; and
- investors receive **complete disclosure** about the investment product before purchase.

In 2017, through their aggressive vigilance, they brought 1,369 disciplinary actions against registered brokers and firms. They levied $64.9 million in fines. And they ordered $66.8 million in restitution to harmed investors they also referred more than 850 fraud and insider trading cases to the SEC and other agencies for litigation and/or prosecution.

FINRA's technology is vital to protecting investors—and has become a key component of their ability to:

- effectively oversee brokerage firms;
- accurately monitor the U.S. equities markets;
- quickly detect potential fraud; and
- keep investors informed through tools like BrokerCheck.

Consumer Financial Protection Bureau (CFPB)

https://www.consumerfinance.gov - The CFPB aims to make consumer financial markets work for consumers, responsible providers and the economy as a whole. They protect consumers from unfair, deceptive or abusive practices and take action against companies that break the law. The CFPB arms people with the information, steps, and tools that they need to make smart financial decisions.

In a market that works, the prices, risks and terms of the deal are clear right up front, so consumers can understand their options and comparison shop. Companies all play by the same consumer protection rules and compete fairly on providing quality and service. To achieve this vision, the CFPB works to:

Empower

They create tools, answer common questions and provide tips that help consumers navigate their financial choices and shop for the deal that works best for them.

Enforce

They act against predatory companies and practices that violate the law and have already returned billions of dollars to harmed consumers.

Educate

They encourage financial education and capability from childhood through retirement, publish research and educate financial companies about their responsibilities.

Investopedia

https://en.wikipedia.org/wiki/Investopedia - **Investopedia** is an American website based in New York City that focuses on investing and finance education along with reviews, ratings and comparisons of various financial products such as brokerage accounts.

Compound Interest Calculator

https://www.investor.gov/additional-resources/free-financial-planning-tools/compound-interest-calculator - Determine how much your money can grow using the power of compound interest.

Saving and Investing – USA.GOV

https://www.usa.gov/saving-investing - Learn how to budget to reach your savings goals. Get the basics on a variety of investments, including savings bonds and other Treasury securities backed by the federal government.

Investments and Grants – Federal Trade Commission (FTC)

https://www.consumer.ftc.gov/topics/investments-grants - Do your research before you commit to an alternative investment or money-making opportunity. Promises of "free money," mysterious financial models and outsized returns are most likely scams.

Federal Deposit Insurance Corporation (FDIC)

https://www.fdic.gov - The Federal Deposit Insurance Corporation (FDIC) preserves and promotes public confidence in the U.S. financial system by insuring deposits in banks and thrift institutions for at least $250,000, by identifying, monitoring and addressing risks to the deposit insurance funds, and by limiting the effect on the economy and the financial system when a bank or thrift institution fails.

An independent agency of the federal government, the FDIC was created in 1933 in response to the thousands of bank failures that occurred in the 1920s and early 1930s. Since the start of FDIC insurance on January 1, 1934, no depositor has lost a single cent of insured funds as a result of a failure.

Glossary

-A -

Alpha - The amount of return expected from an investment from its inherent value.

Alternative Minimum Tax (AMT) - Federal tax, revamped by the Tax Reform Act of 1986, aimed at ensuring that wealthy individuals, trusts, estates, and corporations pay at least some tax.

Annual report - The yearly audited record of a corporation or a mutual fund's condition and performance that is distributed to shareholders.

Annualized - A procedure where figures covering a period of less than one year are extended to cover a 12-month period.

Annualized rate of return - The average annual return over a period of years, considering the effect of compounding. Annualized rate of return also can be called compound growth rate.

Appreciation - The increase in value of a financial asset.

Asset allocation - The process of dividing investments among cash, income, and growth buckets to optimize the balance between risk and reward based on investment needs.

Asset class - Securities with similar features. The most

common asset classes are stocks, bonds, and cash equivalents.

Average maturity - For a bond fund, the average of the stated maturity dates of the debt securities in the portfolio. Also called average weighted maturity. In general, the longer the average maturity, the greater the fund's sensitivity to interest-rate changes, which means greater price fluctuation. A shorter average maturity usually means a less sensitive - and consequently, less volatile - portfolio.

- B -

Balanced fund - Mutual funds that seek both growth and income in a portfolio with a mix of common stock, preferred stock, or bonds. The companies selected typically are in different industries and different geographic regions.

Bear market - A bear market is a prolonged period of falling stock prices, usually marked by a decline of 20% or more. A market in which prices decline sharply against a background of widespread pessimism, growing unemployment or business recession. The opposite of a bull market.

Benchmark - A standard, usually an unmanaged index, used for comparative purposes in assessing performance of a portfolio or mutual fund.

Beta - A measurement of volatility where 1 is neutral;

above 1 is more volatile; and less than 1 is less volatile.

Blue chip - A high-quality, relatively low-risk investment; the term usually refers to stocks of large, well-established companies that have performed well over a long period. The term Blue Chip is borrowed from poker, where the blue chips are the most valuable.

Board of Trustees - A governing board elected or appointed to direct the policies of an institution.

Bond - A bond acts like a loan or an IOU that is issued by a corporation, municipality, or the U.S. government. The issuer promises to repay the full amount of the loan on a specific date and pay a specified rate of return for the use of the money to the investor at specific time intervals.

Bond fund - A mutual fund that invests exclusively in bonds.

Breakpoint - The level of dollar investment in a mutual fund at which an investor becomes eligible for a discounted sales fee. This level may be achieved through a single purchase or a series of smaller purchases.

Bull market - Any market in which prices are advancing in an upward trend. In general, someone is bullish if they believe the value of a security or market will rise. The opposite of a bear market.

- C -

Capital - The funds invested in a company on a long-term

basis and obtained by issuing preferred or common stock, by retaining a portion of the company's earnings from date of incorporation and by long-term borrowing.

Capital gain - The difference between a security's purchase price and its selling price, when the difference is positive.

Capital gains ex-date - The date that a shareholder is no longer eligible for a capital gain distribution that has been declared by a security or mutual fund.

Capital gains long term - The difference between an asset's purchase price and selling price (when the difference is positive) that was earned in more than one year.

Capital gains reinvest NAV - The difference between an asset's purchase price and selling price (when the difference is positive) that was automatically in vested in more shares of the security or mutual fund invested at the security's net asset value.

Capital gains short term - The difference between an asset's purchase price and selling price (when the difference is positive) that was earned in under one year.

Capital loss - The amount by which the proceeds from a sale of a security are less than its purchase price.

Capitalization - The market value of a company, calculated by multiplying the number of shares outstanding by the price per share.

Cash equivalent - A short-term money-market instrument,

such as a Treasury bill or repurchase agreement, of such high liquidity and safety that it is easily converted into cash.

Common stock - Securities that represent ownership in a corporation; must be issued by a corporation.

Contingent deferred sales charge (CDSC) - A back-end sales charge imposed when shares are redeemed from a fund. This fee usually declines over time.

Corporate bond - A long-term bond issued by a corporation to raise outside capital.

Country breakdown - Breakdown of securities in a portfolio by country.

Custodian - A bank that holds a mutual fund's assets, settles all portfolio trades, and collects most of the valuation data required to calculate a fund's net asset value (NAV).

Cut-off time - The time of day when a transaction can no longer be accepted for that trading day.

- D -

Daily dividend factor (date) - Daily dividend distributed by a money market mutual fund.

Default - Failure of a debtor to make timely payments of interest and principal as they come due or to meet some other provision of a bond indenture.

Distribution schedule - A tentative distribution schedule of a mutual fund's dividends and capital gains.

Diversification - The process of owning different investments that tend to perform well at different times in order to reduce the effects of volatility in a portfolio and increase the potential for increasing returns.

Dividend - A dividend is a portion of a company's profit paid to common and preferred shareholders. Dividends provide an incentive to own stock in stable companies even if they are not experiencing much growth. Companies are not required to pay dividends.

Dividend paid - Amount paid to the shareholder of record a security or mutual fund.

Dividend reinvest NAV - Dividends paid to the shareholder of record that are automatically invested in more shares of the security or mutual fund that are purchased at the security's net asset value.

Dividend yield - Annual percentage of return earned by a mutual fund. The yield is determined by dividing the amount of the annual dividends per share by the current net asset value or public offering price.

Dollar cost averaging - Investing the same amount of money at regular intervals over an extended period, regardless of the share price. By investing a fixed amount, you purchase more shares when prices are low, and fewer shares when prices are high. This may reduce your overall average cost of investing.

Dow Jones Industrial Average (Dow) - The most commonly used indicator of stock market performance, based on prices of 30 actively traded blue chip stocks, primarily major industrial companies. The Average is the sum of the current market price of 30 major industrial companies' stocks divided by a number that has been adjusted to consider stocks splits and changes in stock composition.

- E -

EPS - The portion of a company's profit allocated to each outstanding share of common stock. EPS serves as an indicator of a company's profitability.

Equities - Shares issued by a company which represent ownership in it. Ownership of property, usually in the form of common stocks, as distinguished from fixed-income securities such as bonds or mortgages. Stock funds may vary depending on the fund's investment objective.

Equity fund - A mutual fund/collective fund in which the money is invested primarily in common and/or preferred stock. Stock funds may vary, depending on the fund's investment objective.

Ex-Dividend - The interval between the announcement and the payment of the next dividend for a stock.

Ex-Dividend date - The date on which a stock goes ex-dividend. Typically, about three weeks before the dividend is paid to shareholders of record.

Exchange privilege - The ability to transfer money from one mutual fund to another within the same fund family.

Expense ratio - The ratio between a mutual fund's operating expenses for the year and the average value of its net assets.

Expense ratio (date) - Amount, expressed as a percentage of total investment that shareholders pay annually for mutual fund operating expenses and management fees.

- F -

Federal Funds Rate (Fed Funds Rate) - The interest rate charged by banks with excess reserves at a Federal Reserve district bank to banks needing overnight loans to meet reserve requirements. The most sensitive indicator of the direction of interest rates, since it is set daily by the market, unlike the prime rate and the discount rate, which are periodically changed by banks and by the Federal Reserve Board.

Federal Reserve Board (The Fed) - The governing board of the Federal Reserve System, it regulates the nation's money supply by setting the discount rate, tightening, or easing the availability of credit in the economy.

Fixed income fund - A fund or portfolio where bonds are primarily purchased as investments. There is no fixed maturity date and no repayment guarantee.

Fixed income security - A security that pays a set rate of interest on a regular basis.

Fund - A pool of money from a group of investors in order to buy securities. The two major ways funds may be offered are (1) by companies in the securities business (these funds are called mutual funds); and (2) by bank trust departments (these are called collective funds).

- G -

Growth investing - Investment strategy that focuses on stocks of companies and stock funds where earnings are growing rapidly and are expected to continue growing.

Growth stock - Typically a well-known, successful company that is experiencing rapid growth in earnings and revenue, and usually pays little or no dividend.

Growth-style funds - Growth funds focus on future gains. A growth fund manager will typically invest in stocks with earnings that outperform the current market. The manager attempts to achieve success by focusing on rapidly growing sectors of the economy and investing in leading companies with consistent earnings growth. The fund grows primarily as individual share prices climb.

- I -

Index - An investment index tracks the performance of many investments as a way of measuring the overall performance of a particular investment type or category. The S&P 500 is widely considered the benchmark for large-stock investors. It tracks the performance of 500 large U.S. company stocks.

Individual Retirement Account (IRA) - A tax-deferred account to which an eligible individual can make annual contributions up to $3,000 ($6,000 for a single-income married couple filing a joint income tax return).

Inflation - A rise in the prices of goods and services, often equated with loss of purchasing power.

Interest rate - The fixed amount of money that an issuer agrees to pay the bondholders. It is most often a percentage of the face value of the bond. Interest rates constitute one of the self-regulating mechanisms of the market, falling in response to economic weakness and rising on strength.

Interest-rate risk - The possibility of a reduction in the value of a security, especially a bond, resulting from a rise in interest rates.

Investment advisor - An organization employed by a mutual fund to give professional advice on the fund's investments and asset management practices.

Investment company - A corporation, trust or partnership that invests pooled shareholder dollars in securities appropriate to the organization's objective. Mutual funds, closed-end funds and unit investment trusts are the three types of investment companies.

Investment grade bonds - A bond generally considered suitable for purchase by prudent investors.

Investment objective - The goal of a mutual fund and its shareholders, e.g. growth, growth and income, income, and tax-free income.

- J -

Junk bond - A lower-rated, usually higher-yielding bond, with a credit rating of BB or lower.

- L -

Large-cap - The market capitalization of the stocks of companies with market values greater than $10 billion.

Letter of intent - A letter of intent may also be issued by a mutual fund shareholder to indicate that he/she would like to invest certain amounts of money at certain specified times. In exchange for signing a letter of intent, the shareholder would often qualify for reduced sales charges. A letter of intent is not a contract and cannot be enforced, it is just a document stating serious intent to carry out certain business activities.

Lipper ratings - The Lipper Mutual Fund Industry Average is the performance level of all mutual funds, as reported by Lipper Analytical Services of New York. The performance of all mutual funds is ranked quarterly and annually, by type of fund such as aggressive growth fund or income fund. Mutual fund managers try to beat the industry average as well as the other funds in their category.

Liquidity - The ability to have ready access to invested

money. Mutual funds are liquid because their shares can be redeemed for current value (which may be more or less than the original cost) on any business day.

Loads (back-end, front-end and no-load) - Sales charges on mutual funds. A back-end load is assessed at redemption (see contingent deferred sales charge), while a front-end load is paid at the time of purchase. No-load funds are free of sales charges.

Long-term investment strategy - A strategy that looks past the day-to-day fluctuations of the stock and bond markets and responds to fundamental changes in the financial markets or the economy.

- M -

Management fee - The amount paid by a mutual fund to the investment advisor for its services.

Market price - The current price of an asset.

Market risk - The possibility that an investment will not achieve its target.

Market timing - A risky investment strategy that calls for buying and selling securities in anticipation of market conditions.

Maturity - The date specified in a note or bond on which the debt is due and payable.

Maturity distribution - The breakdown of a portfolio's assets based on the time frame when the investments will mature.

Median Market Cap - The midpoint of market capitalization (market price multiplied by the number of shares outstanding) of the stocks in a portfolio, where half the stocks have higher market capitalization and half have lower.

Mid-cap - The market capitalization of the stocks of companies with market values between $3 to $10 billion.

Money market mutual fund - A short-term investment that seeks to protect principal and generate income by investing in Treasury bills, CDs with maturities less than one year and other conservative investments.

Morningstar ratings - System for rating open- and closed-end mutual funds and annuities by Morningstar Inc. of Chicago. The system rates funds from one to five stars, using a risk-adjusted performance rating in which performance equals total return of the fund.

Mutual fund - Fund operated by an investment company that raises money from shareholders and invests it in stocks, bonds, options, commodities, or money market securities.

- N -

NASDAQ - National Association of Securities Dealers Automated Quotations system, which is owned and operated by the National Association of Securities Dealers. NASDAQ is a computerized system that provides brokers and dealers with price quotations for securities traded over the counter as well as for many New York Stock Exchange listed securities.

Net Asset Value per share (NAV) - The current dollar value of a single mutual fund share; also known as share price. The fund's NAV is calculated daily by taking the fund's total assets, subtracting the fund's liabilities, and dividing by the number of shares outstanding. The NAV does not include the sales charge. The process of calculating the NAV is called pricing.

Number of Holdings - Total number of individual securities in a fund or portfolio.

- P -

P/B Ratio - The price per share of a stock divided by its book value (net worth) per share. For a stock portfolio, the ratio is the weighted average price-to-book ratio of the stocks it holds.

Par value - Par value is the amount originally paid for a bond and the amount that will be repaid at maturity. Bonds are typically sold in multiples of $1,000.

Portfolio - A collection of investments owned by one organization or individual and managed as a collective whole with specific investment goals in mind.

Portfolio allocation - Amount of assets in a portfolio specifically designated for a certain type of investment.

Portfolio holdings - Investments included in a portfolio.

Portfolio manager - The person or entity responsible for making investment decisions of the portfolio to meet the specific investment objective or goal of the portfolio.

Preferred stock - A class of stock with a fixed dividend that has preference over a company's common stock in the payment of dividends and the liquidation of assets. There are several kinds of preferred stock, among them adjustable-rate and convertible.

Premium - The amount by which a bond or stock sells above its par value.

Price-to-book - The price per share of a stock divided by its book value (net worth) per share. For a stock portfolio, the ratio is the weighted average price-to-book ratio of the stocks it holds.

Price-to-earnings (P/E) Ratio - A stock's price divided by its earnings per share, which indicates how much investors are paying for a company's earning power.

P/E Ratio (1 yr. trailing) (long position) - Price of a stock divided by its earnings from the latest year.

P/E Ratio (1 yr. forecast) - Price of a stock divided by its projected earnings for the coming year.

Prospectus - Formal written offer to sell securities that sets forth the plan for proposed business enterprise or the facts concerning an existing one that an investor needs to make an informed decision. Prospectuses are also issued by mutual funds, containing information required by the SEC, such as history, background of managers, fund objectives and policies, financial statement, risks, services and fees.

Proxy - A shareholder vote on matters that require shareholders' approval.

Public offering price (POP) - A mutual fund share's purchase price, including sales charges.

- Q -

Quality distribution - The breakdown of a portfolio's assets based on quality rating of the investments.

- R -

R2 - The percentage of a fund's movements that result from movements in the index ranging from 0 to 100. A fund with an R2 of 100 means that 100 percent of the fund's movement can completely be explained by movements in the fund's external index benchmark.

Ratings - Evaluations of the credit quality of bonds usually made by independent rating services. Ratings generally measure the probability of timely repayment of principal and interest on debt securities.

Recession - A downturn in economic activity, defined by many economists as at least two consecutive quarters of decline in a country's gross domestic product.

Redemption - Sale of mutual fund shares by a shareholder.

Reinvestment option - Refers to an arrangement under which a mutual fund will apply dividends or capital gains distributions for its shareholders toward the purchase of additional shares.

Relative risk and potential return - The amount of potential return from an investment as related to the amount of risk you are willing to accept.

Rights of accumulation - The right to buy over a period. For example, this might be done by an institutional investor to avoid making a single substantial purchase that might drive up the market price, or by a retail investor who wants to reduce risk by dollar cost averaging.

Risk tolerance - The degree to which you can tolerate volatility in your investment values.

- S -

Sales charge - An amount charged for the sale of some fund shares, usually those sold by brokers or other sales professionals. By regulation, a mutual fund sales charge may not exceed 8.5 percent of an investment purchase. The charge may vary depending on the amount invested and the fund chosen. A sales charge or load is reflected in the asked or offering price. See loads.

Sector - A group of similar securities, such as equities in a specific industry.

Sector breakdown - Breakdown of securities in a portfolio by industry categories.

Securities - Another name for investments such as stocks or bonds. The name 'securities' comes from the documents that certify an investor's ownership of stocks or bonds.

Securities and Exchange Commission (SEC) - The federal agency created by the Securities and Exchange Act of 1934 that administers the laws governing the securities industry, including the registration and distribution of mutual fund shares.

Share - A unit of ownership in an investment, such as a share of a stock or a mutual fund.

Share class net assets (date) - Fund assets included in a specific share class.

Share classes - Classes represent ownership in the same fund but charge different fees. This can enable shareholders to choose the type of fee structure that best suits their needs.

Sharpe Ratio - A risk-adjusted measure that measures reward per unit of risk. The higher the Sharpe ratio, the better. The numerator is the difference between the Fund's annualized return and the annualized return of the risk-free instrument (T-Bills).

Short-term investment - Asset purchased with an

investment life of less than a year.

Small-cap - The market capitalization of the stocks of companies with market values less than $3 billion.

Standard & Poor's Index - Broad-based measurement of changes in stock market conditions based on the average performance of 500 widely held common stocks commonly known as the Standard & Poor's 500 or S&P 500.

Standard Deviation - A statistical measure of the degree to which an individual value in a probability distribution tends to vary from the mean of the distribution.

Statement of additional information (SAI) - The supplementary document to a prospectus that contains more detailed information about a mutual fund; also known as 'Part B' of the prospectus.

Stock - A long-term, growth-oriented investment representing ownership in a company; also known as 'equity.'

Stockholder - The owner of common or preferred stock of a corporation. Also called 'shareholder.'

Systematic investment plan - A service option that allows investors to buy mutual fund shares on a regular schedule, usually through bank account deductions.

- T -

Tax-exempt income - Tax-exempt income is income that is

exempt from income taxes. A purchaser of state municipal bonds is exempt from federal taxation on the income earned from the bonds.

Time horizon - The amount of time that you expect to stay invested in an asset or security.

Top 10 holdings - Ten largest holdings in a portfolio based on asset value.

Top 10 long and short positions - The top 10 holdings ranked by market value in each position category (long and short). A long position is one in which an investor buys shares of stock and as an equity holder will profit if the price of the stock rises. With a short position an investor will sell shares of stock that they do not own but have borrowed. The investor in a short position will profit if the price of the stock falls.

Top five contributors - Five assets in a portfolio that generated largest negative returns (losses).

Top five detractors - Top five industries in a portfolio based on amount of invested assets.

Top five holdings - Top five securities in a portfolio based on amount of invested assets.

Top five industries - Top five industries in a portfolio based on amount of invested assets.

Total return - Accounts for all the dividends and interest earned before deductions for fees and expenses, in addition to any changes in the value of the principal, including share price, assuming the funds' dividends and capital gains are reinvested. Often, this percentage is presented in a specified period (one, five, ten years and/or life of fund). Also, a method of calculating an investment's return that takes share price changes and dividends into account.

Tracking Error - The active risk of the portfolio. It determines the annualized standard deviation of the excess returns between the portfolio and the benchmark.

Transfer agent - An agent, usually a commercial bank, appointed to monitor records of stocks, bonds and shareholders. A transfer agent keeps a record of the name of each registered shareholder, his or her address, the number of shares owned, and sees that certificates presented for the transfer are properly canceled and new certificates are issued in the name of the new owner.

Treasury bill - Negotiable short-term (one year or less) debt obligations issued by the U.S. government and backed by its full faith and credit.

Treasury bond - Negotiable long-term (10 years or longer) debt obligations issued by the U.S. government and backed by its full faith and credit.

Treasury note - Negotiable medium-term (one year to 10 years) debt obligations issued by the U.S. government and backed by its full faith and credit.

Treasury security - Securities issued by the U.S. Treasury Department and backed by the U.S. government.

Trustee - 1. An organization or individual who has responsibility for one or more accounts. 2. An individual who, as part of a fund's board of trustees, has ultimate responsibility for a fund's activities.

Turnover Ratio - Percentage of holdings in a mutual fund that are sold in a specified period.

- V -

Valuation - An estimate of the value or worth of a company; the price investors assign to an individual stock.

Value investing - A strategy whereby investors purchase equity securities that they believe are selling below estimated true value. The investor can profit by buying these securities then selling them once they appreciate to their real value.

Value stock - Typically an overlooked or underpriced company that is growing at slower rates.

Value-style funds - Value-style funds typically hold company stocks that are undervalued in the market. Fundamentally strong companies whose stocks are inexpensive, but trending upward may also be selected for value funds.

Volatility - The amount and frequency with which an investment fluctuates in value.

- W -

Wtd. Avg. Market Cap - Most indexes are constructed by weighting the market capitalization of each stock on the index. In such an index, larger companies account for a greater portion of the index. An example is the S&P 500 Index.

Weighted average maturity - A Fund's WAM calculates an average time to maturity of all the securities held in the portfolio, weighted by each security's percentage of net assets. The calculation considers the final maturity for a fixed income security and the interest rate reset date for floating rate securities held in the portfolio. This is a way to measure a fund's sensitivity to potential interest rate changes.

- Y -

YTD total return - Year-to-date return on an investment including appreciation and dividends or interest.

YTD - Year-to-date return on an investment including appreciation and dividends or interest.

YTD Return (w load) - Year-to-date return on an investment including appreciation and dividends or interest, minus any applicable expenses or charges.

Yield - Annual percentage rate of return on capital. The dividend or interest paid by a company expressed as a percentage of the current price.

Yield to maturity - Concept used to determine the rate of

return an investor will receive if a long-term, interest-bearing investment, such as a bond, is held to its maturity date.

Yield to maturity distribution - The average rate of return that will be earned on a bond if held to maturity.

- # -

12b-1 fee - A mutual fund fee, named for the SEC rule that permits it, used to pay for broker-dealer compensation and other distribution costs. If a fund has a 12b-1 fee, it will be disclosed in the fee table of the fund's prospectus.

30-day SEC yield (date) - Represents net investment income earned by a fund over a 30-day period, expressed as an annual percentage rate based on the fund's share price at the end of the 30-day period. The 30-day yield should be regarded as an estimate of investment income and may not equal the fund's actual income distribution rate.

52 Week High - A security's trading high point over the last 52-week period.

52 Week Low - A security's trading low point over the last 52-week period.

ABOUT THE AUTHOR

Mark A. Parks, Jr. and his wife Connie own MarCon Consulting, a financial services company that has helped hundreds of individuals and companies with financial strategies, accounting, and organizational design for over twenty-five years

Mark has served as CFO for the 29th largest county in America (there are more than 3,000 counties in America) and he has managed the finances for one of America's fastest growing cities. During his professional career Mark has realized the severe disparities in people's lives, especially women and he noted the difference centered around financial resources. The discovery contributed to Mark's decision to write this book that focuses on women and investing. Mark embarked on this quest years ago after realizing his sister, an extremely well-educated person earning a high salary didn't understand principles of investing. When he asked other women about investing, he discovered the need for this information was great and it was not related to any one demographic. Having read statistics that show nine of ten women will be responsible for their household finances at some point in their lives, Mark and Connie saw a huge opportunity to help improve the outcome of families. Educating women in mass could have an exponential impact on America's family's finances.

Mark served as the financial expert for the CBS affiliate in Cleveland, Ohio, WOIO, informing audiences about the impacts of the financial markets and he has spoken at hundreds of financial seminars including periodic Women and Investing Seminars. Mark's caring approach has helped him get access to women who willingly share concerns about their most challenging financial issues and then trust Mark to help guide them through the challenges.

Mark graduated from Baldwin Wallace University with a BA Degree and the University of Phoenix with an MBA. He holds a life insurance license and he is a Certified Public Accountant.

Made in the USA
Las Vegas, NV
08 December 2021